HEROIC ANIMALS

CHER AMI COMES THROUGH

HEROIC CARRIER PIGEON OF WORLD WAR I

BY **NEL YOMTOV**   ILLUSTRATED BY **MARK SIMMONS**

CAPSTONE PRESS
a capstone imprint

Published by Capstone Press, an imprint of Capstone.
1710 Roe Crest Drive, North Mankato, Minnesota 56003
capstonepub.com

Library of Congress Cataloging-in-Publication Data
Names: Yomtov, Nel, author. | Simmons, Mark, illustrator.
Title: Cher Ami comes through : heroic carrier pigeon of World War I / by
   Nel Yomtov ; illustrated by Mark Simmons.
Description: North Mankato, Minnesota : Capstone Press, an imprint of Capstone, [2023] |
   Series: Heroic animals | Includes bibliographical references. | Audience: Ages 8-11 |
   Audience: Grades 4-6 |
Summary: "In October 1918, World War I had been raging in Europe for more than four
   years. When Major Charles Whittlesey led the U.S. 77th Division into France's Argonne
   Forest, his troops were soon surrounded and cut off from escape by German forces.
   Things became even more dangerous when the division came under friendly fire from
   U.S. forces. The troops' only hope was to send a carrier pigeon named Cher Ami with a
   desperate message to stop the attack. Read all about the brave little pigeon that carried
   out a dangerous mission to deliver a desperate message across a deadly battlefield"--
   Provided by publisher.
Identifiers: LCCN 2022024612 (print) | LCCN 2022024613 (ebook) | ISBN 9781666394023
   (hardcover) | ISBN 9781666394030 (paperback) | ISBN 9781666394016 (pdf) |
   ISBN 9781666394054 (kindle edition)
Subjects: LCSH: Cher Ami (Pigeon)--Juvenile literature. | World War, 1914-1918--
   Communications--Juvenile literature. | Homing pigeons--War use--United States--
   History--20th century--Juvenile literature. | Famous animals--United States--Juvenile
   literature.
Classification: LCC D639.P45 Y66 2023 (print) | LCC D639.P45 (ebook) |
   DDC 940.4/12730929--dc23/eng/20220601
LC record available at https://lccn.loc.gov/2022024612
LC ebook record available at https://lccn.loc.gov/2022024613

Editorial Credits
Editor: Aaron Sautter; Designer: Elyse White; Media Researcher: Morgan Walters;
Production Specialist: Whitney Schaefer

Photo Credit
Alamy: 29, Imago History Collection

All internet sites appearing in back matter were available and accurate when this book was
sent to press.

Direct quotes appear in **bold, *italicized*** text on the following pages:

Pages 8, 11, 13, 14, 20 (middle right), 26: Werstein, Irving. *The Lost Battalion: A Saga of
   American Courage in World War I.* New York: W.W. Norton & Company, 1966.
Pages 17, 20 (message): "Notre Cher Ami: The Enduring Myth and Memory of a Humble
   Pigeon," by Frank A. Blazich Jr. *Journal of Military History #5*, July 2021.

Printed and bound in the USA.   PO# 5195

TABLE OF CONTENTS

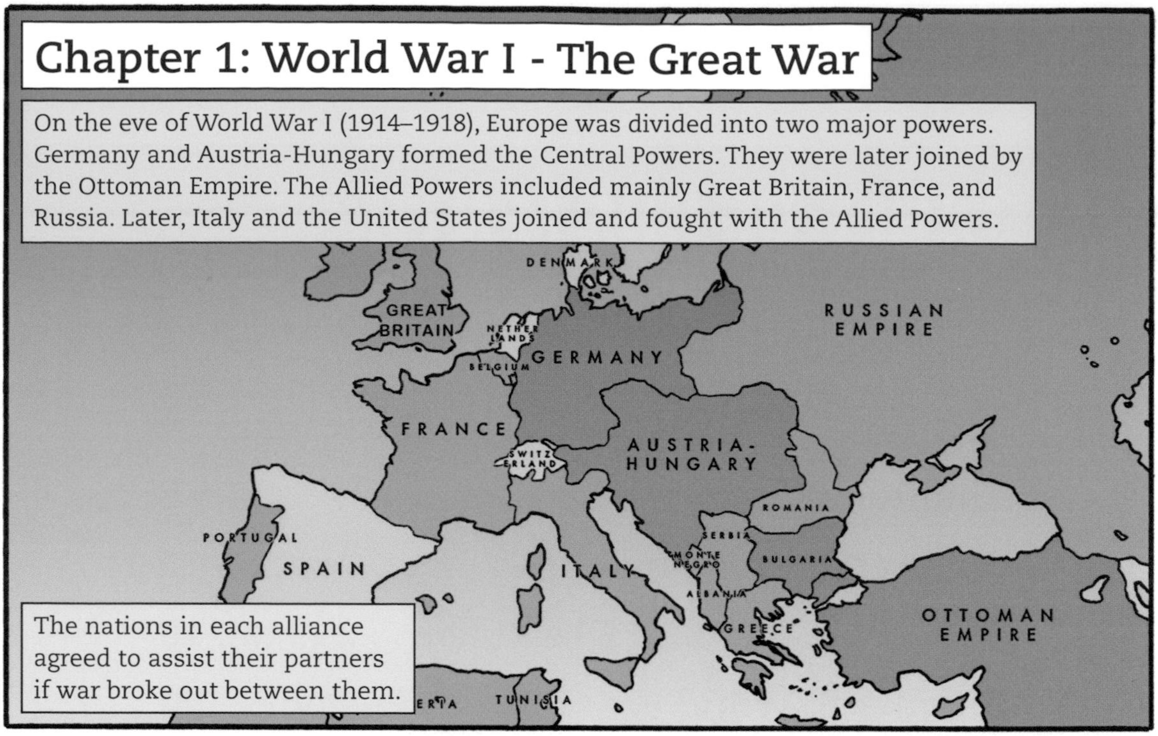
Chapter 1: World War I - The Great War
On the eve of World War I (1914–1918), Europe was divided into two major powers. Germany and Austria-Hungary formed the Central Powers. They were later joined by the Ottoman Empire. The Allied Powers included mainly Great Britain, France, and Russia. Later, Italy and the United States joined and fought with the Allied Powers.
DENMARK
GREAT BRITAIN
NETHERLANDS
BELGIUM
GERMANY
RUSSIAN EMPIRE
FRANCE
SWITZERLAND
AUSTRIA-HUNGARY
ROMANIA
SERBIA
MONTENEGRO
BULGARIA
PORTUGAL
SPAIN
ITALY
ALBANIA
GREECE
OTTOMAN EMPIRE
TUNISIA
The nations in each alliance agreed to assist their partners if war broke out between them.

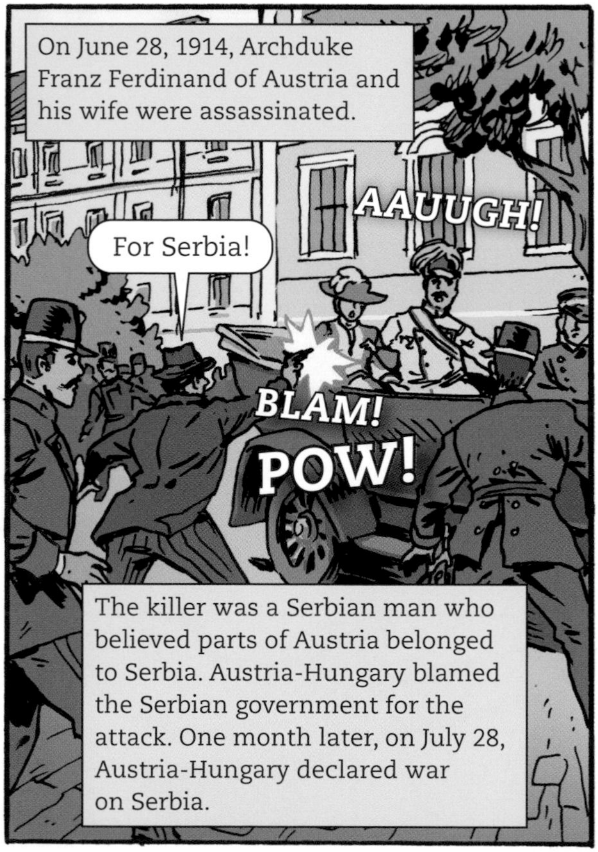
On June 28, 1914, Archduke Franz Ferdinand of Austria and his wife were assassinated.
AAUUGH!
For Serbia!
BLAM!
POW!
The killer was a Serbian man who believed parts of Austria belonged to Serbia. Austria-Hungary blamed the Serbian government for the attack. One month later, on July 28, Austria-Hungary declared war on Serbia.

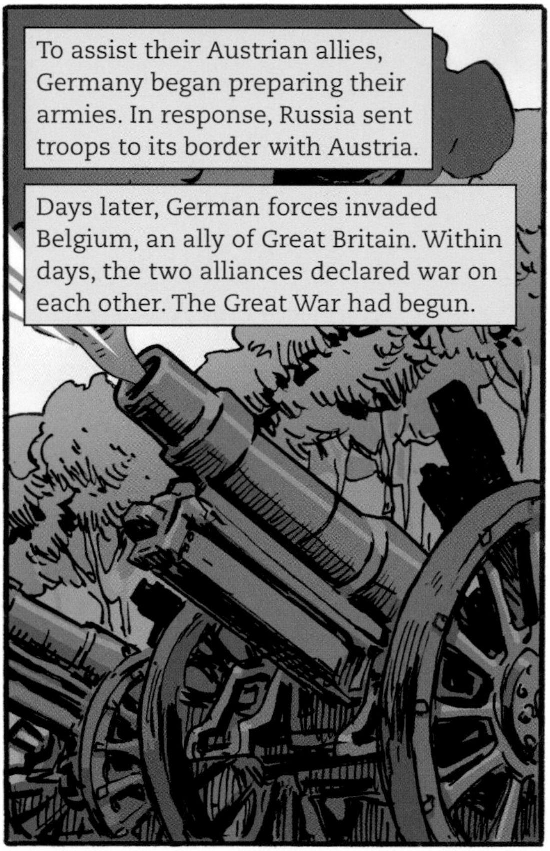
To assist their Austrian allies, Germany began preparing their armies. In response, Russia sent troops to its border with Austria.
Days later, German forces invaded Belgium, an ally of Great Britain. Within days, the two alliances declared war on each other. The Great War had begun.

During the early years of the war, the United States remained neutral. However, several U.S. ships were damaged or sunk by German mines while traveling to Great Britain.

In May 1915, a German submarine sunk the passenger ship *Lusitania*, killing 128 Americans.

AAUUGGH!

BOOOMM!

In February 1917, the U.S. government learned that Germany had secretly tried to get Mexico to attack the United States.

FIRST EDITION

EVENING TRIBUNE WEATHER

GERMANY ADMITS PLOT

TALK IS HEARD IN SENATE DURING DEBATE

EXTRA SESSION

Germany's hostile actions outraged Americans. The public demanded that the U.S. government respond.

On April 6, the United States officially declared war on Germany. By December 1917, 175,000 U.S. soldiers were in Europe.

Riverside Enterprise

U.S. AT WAR!

91 INTERNED GERMAN SHIPS SEIZED

America's First Act of War In Seizure of Big Fleet of Interned Ships

PRESIDENT WILSON SIGNS WAR RESOLUTION/ HOW RADIOS FLASH NEWS TO NAVY AND WORLD

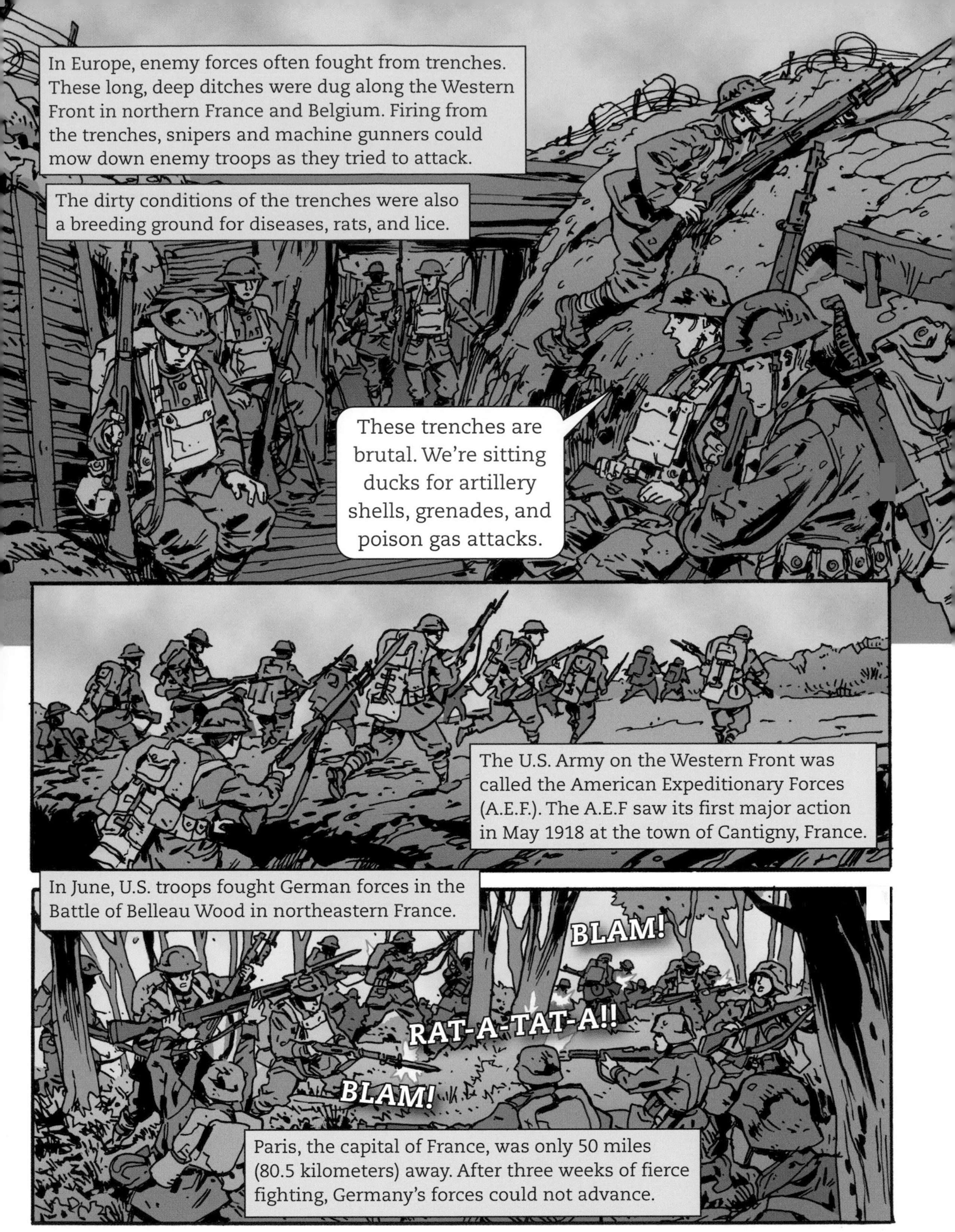
In Europe, enemy forces often fought from trenches. These long, deep ditches were dug along the Western Front in northern France and Belgium. Firing from the trenches, snipers and machine gunners could mow down enemy troops as they tried to attack.
The dirty conditions of the trenches were also a breeding ground for diseases, rats, and lice.
These trenches are brutal. We're sitting ducks for artillery shells, grenades, and poison gas attacks.
The U.S. Army on the Western Front was called the American Expeditionary Forces (A.E.F.). The A.E.F saw its first major action in May 1918 at the town of Cantigny, France.
In June, U.S. troops fought German forces in the Battle of Belleau Wood in northeastern France.
BLAM!
RAT-A-TAT-A!!
BLAM!
Paris, the capital of France, was only 50 miles (80.5 kilometers) away. After three weeks of fierce fighting, Germany's forces could not advance.

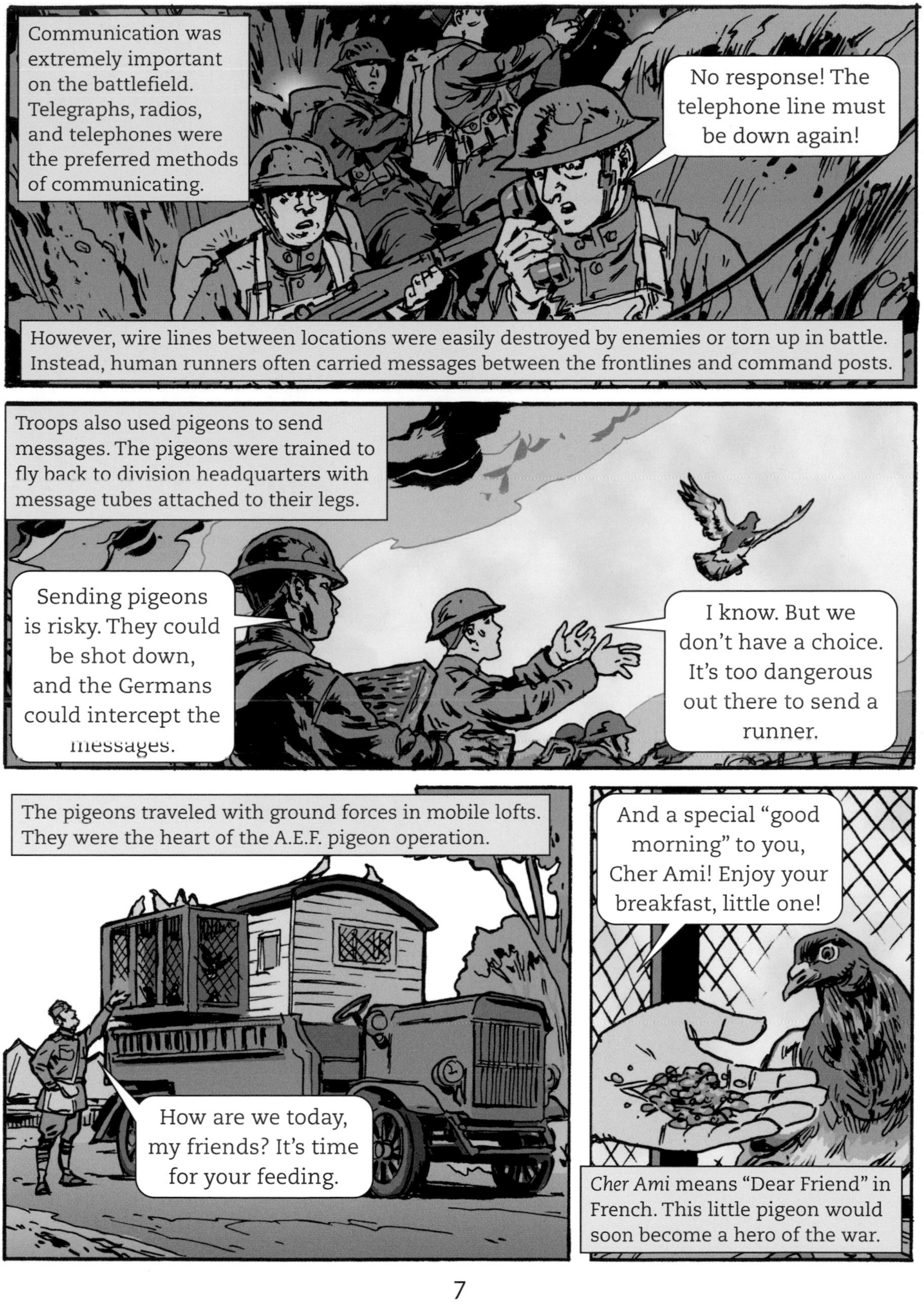
Communication was extremely important on the battlefield. Telegraphs, radios, and telephones were the preferred methods of communicating.
No response! The telephone line must be down again!
However, wire lines between locations were easily destroyed by enemies or torn up in battle. Instead, human runners often carried messages between the frontlines and command posts.
Troops also used pigeons to send messages. The pigeons were trained to fly back to division headquarters with message tubes attached to their legs.
Sending pigeons is risky. They could be shot down, and the Germans could intercept the messages.
I know. But we don't have a choice. It's too dangerous out there to send a runner.
The pigeons traveled with ground forces in mobile lofts. They were the heart of the A.E.F. pigeon operation.
How are we today, my friends? It's time for your feeding.
And a special "good morning" to you, Cher Ami! Enjoy your breakfast, little one!
Cher Ami means "Dear Friend" in French. This little pigeon would soon become a hero of the war.

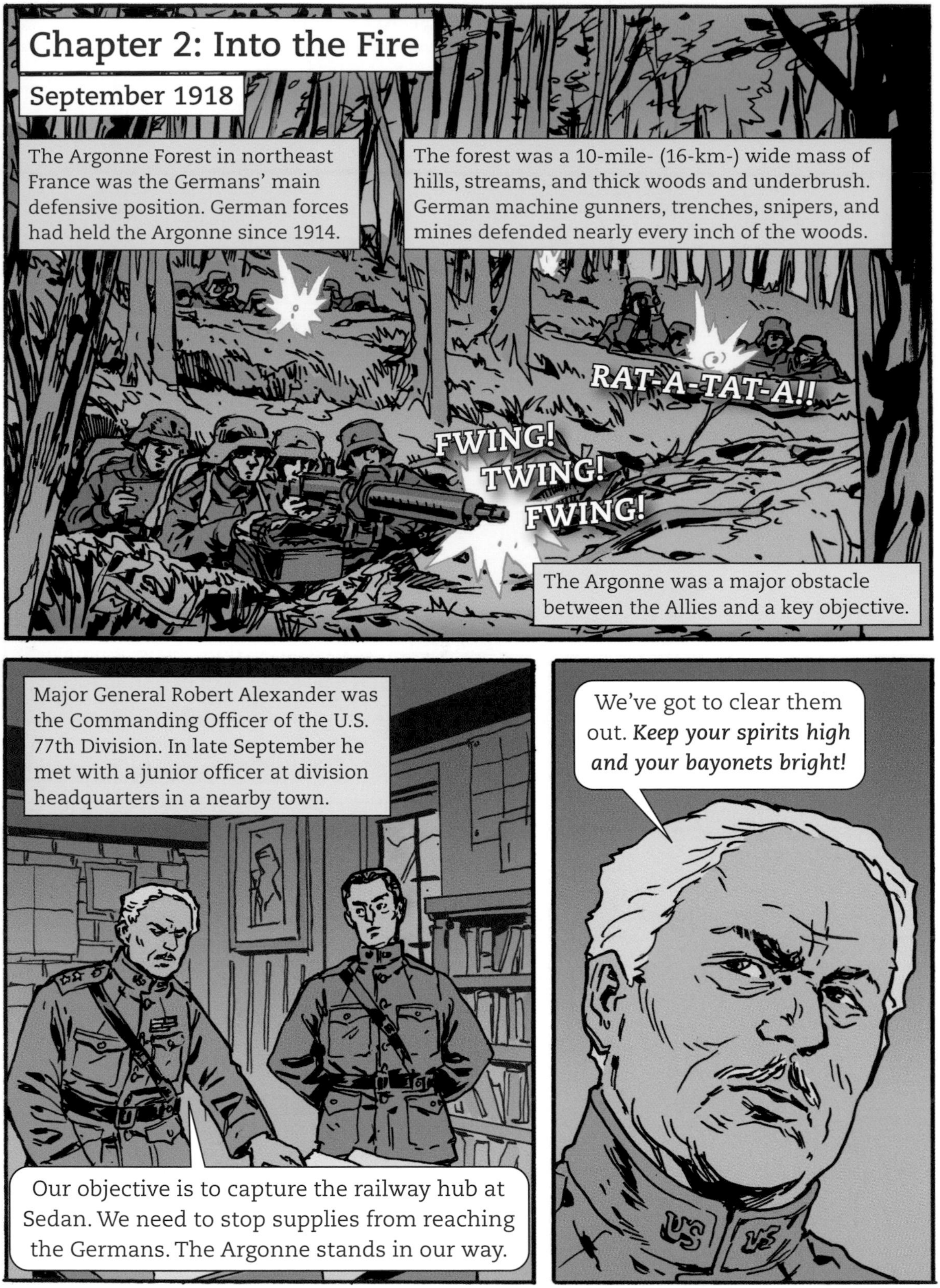
Chapter 2: Into the Fire
September 1918
The Argonne Forest in northeast France was the Germans' main defensive position. German forces had held the Argonne since 1914.
The forest was a 10-mile- (16-km-) wide mass of hills, streams, and thick woods and underbrush. German machine gunners, trenches, snipers, and mines defended nearly every inch of the woods.
RAT-A-TAT-A!!
FWING!
TWING!
FWING!
The Argonne was a major obstacle between the Allies and a key objective.
Major General Robert Alexander was the Commanding Officer of the U.S. 77th Division. In late September he met with a junior officer at division headquarters in a nearby town.
Our objective is to capture the railway hub at Sedan. We need to stop supplies from reaching the Germans. The Argonne stands in our way.
We've got to clear them out. *Keep your spirits high and your bayonets bright!*
US
US

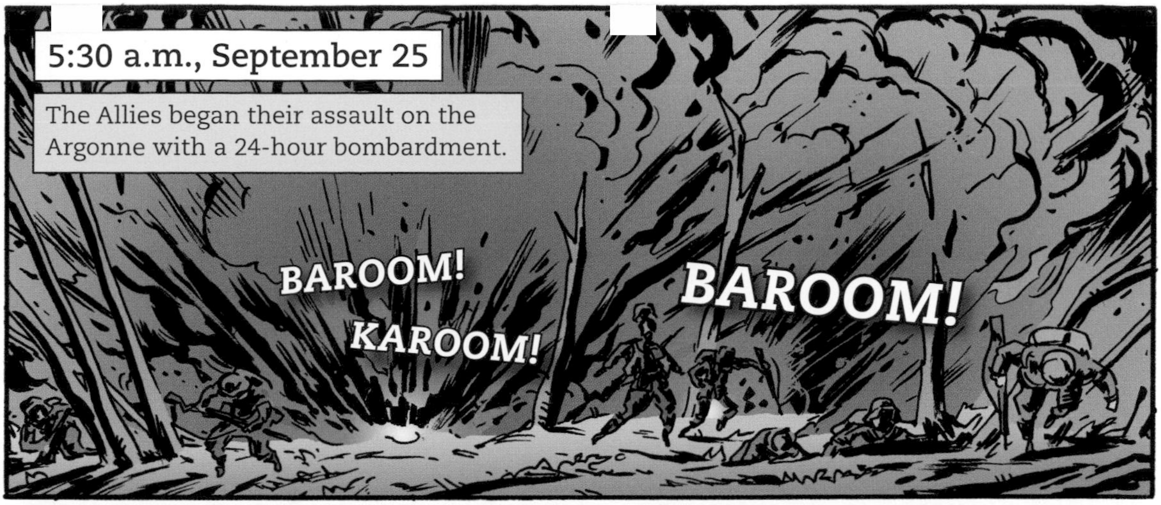
5:30 a.m., September 25
The Allies began their assault on the Argonne with a 24-hour bombardment.
BAROOM!
KAROOM!
BAROOM!

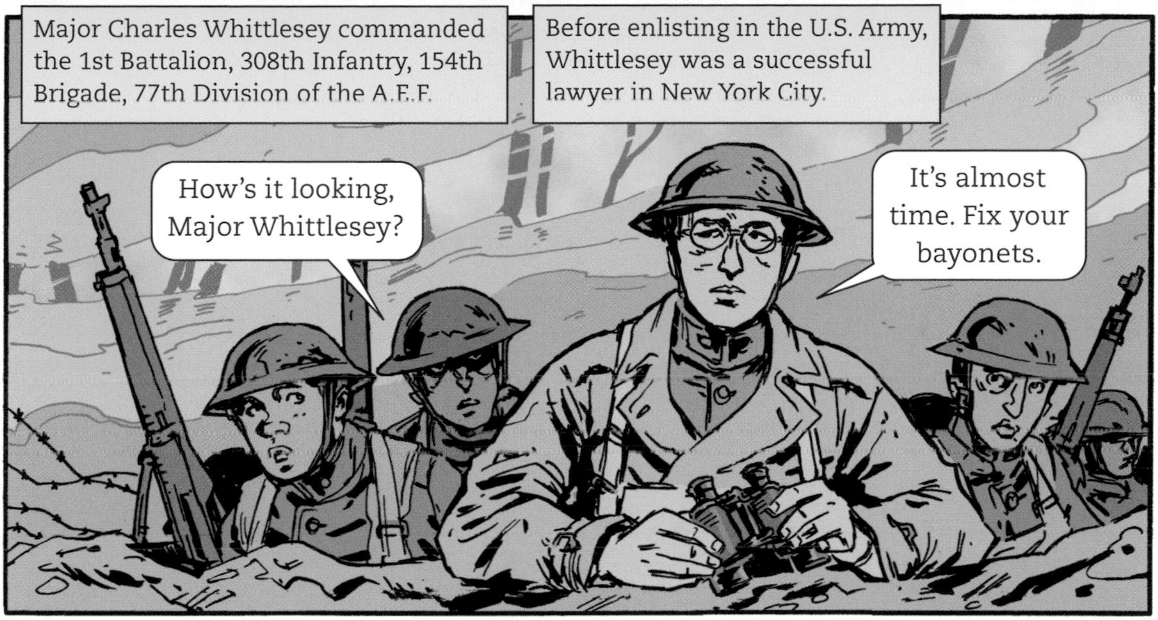
Major Charles Whittlesey commanded the 1st Battalion, 308th Infantry, 154th Brigade, 77th Division of the A.E.F.
Before enlisting in the U.S. Army, Whittlesey was a successful lawyer in New York City.
How's it looking, Major Whittlesey?
It's almost time. Fix your bayonets.

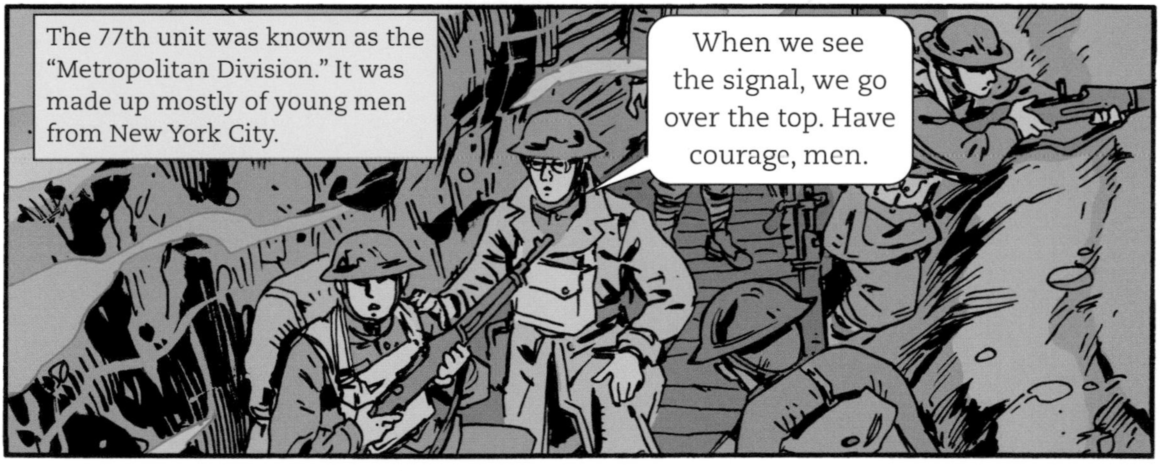
The 77th unit was known as the "Metropolitan Division." It was made up mostly of young men from New York City.
When we see the signal, we go over the top. Have courage, men.

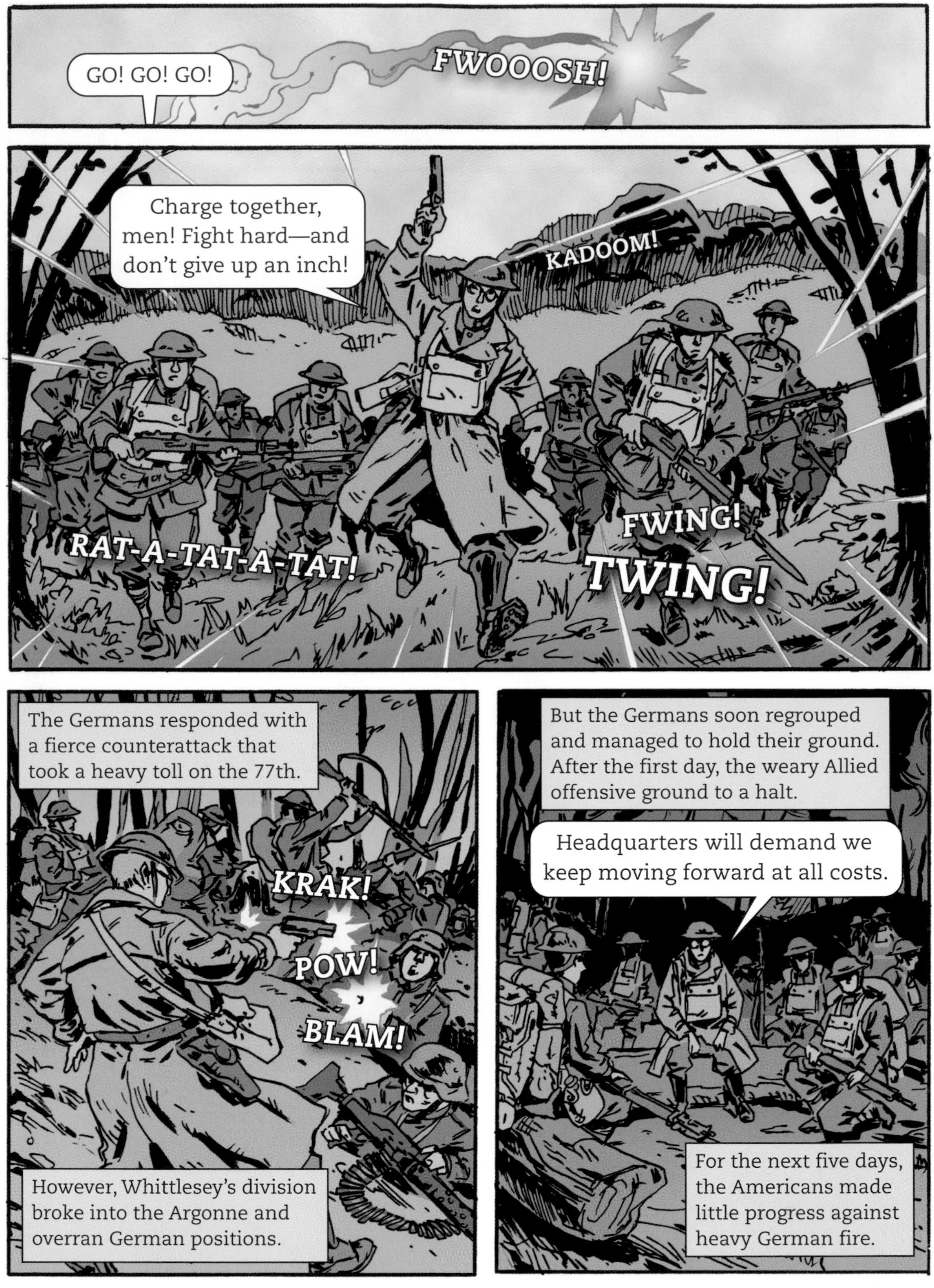

GO! GO! GO!
FWOOOSH!
Charge together, men! Fight hard—and don't give up an inch!
KADOOM!
RAT-A-TAT-A-TAT!
FWING!
TWING!
The Germans responded with a fierce counterattack that took a heavy toll on the 77th.
KRAK!
POW!
BLAM!
However, Whittlesey's division broke into the Argonne and overran German positions.
But the Germans soon regrouped and managed to hold their ground. After the first day, the weary Allied offensive ground to a halt.
Headquarters will demand we keep moving forward at all costs.
For the next five days, the Americans made little progress against heavy German fire.

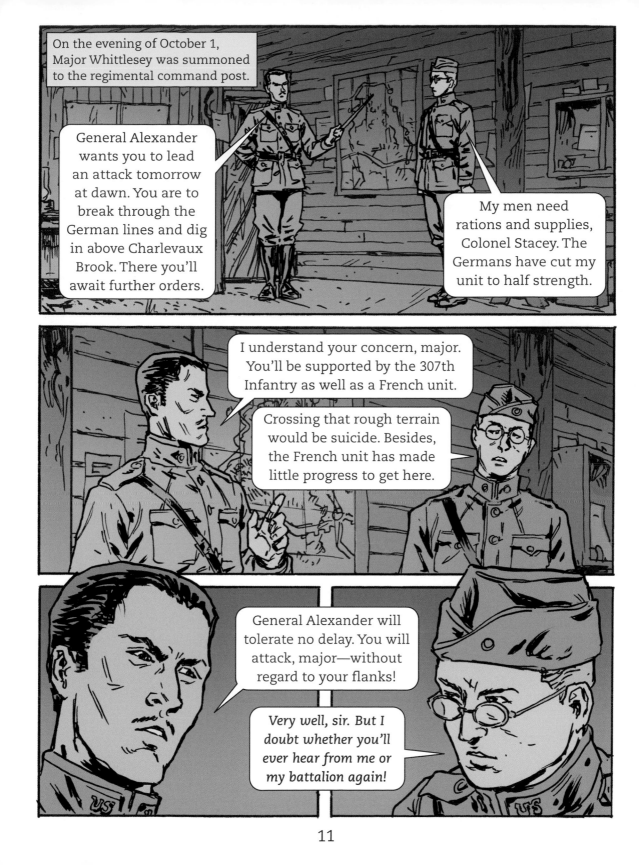

On the evening of October 1, Major Whittlesey was summoned to the regimental command post.

General Alexander wants you to lead an attack tomorrow at dawn. You are to break through the German lines and dig in above Charlevaux Brook. There you'll await further orders.

My men need rations and supplies, Colonel Stacey. The Germans have cut my unit to half strength.

I understand your concern, major. You'll be supported by the 307th Infantry as well as a French unit.

Crossing that rough terrain would be suicide. Besides, the French unit has made little progress to get here.

General Alexander will tolerate no delay. You will attack, major—without regard to your flanks!

Very well, sir. But I doubt whether you'll ever hear from me or my battalion again!

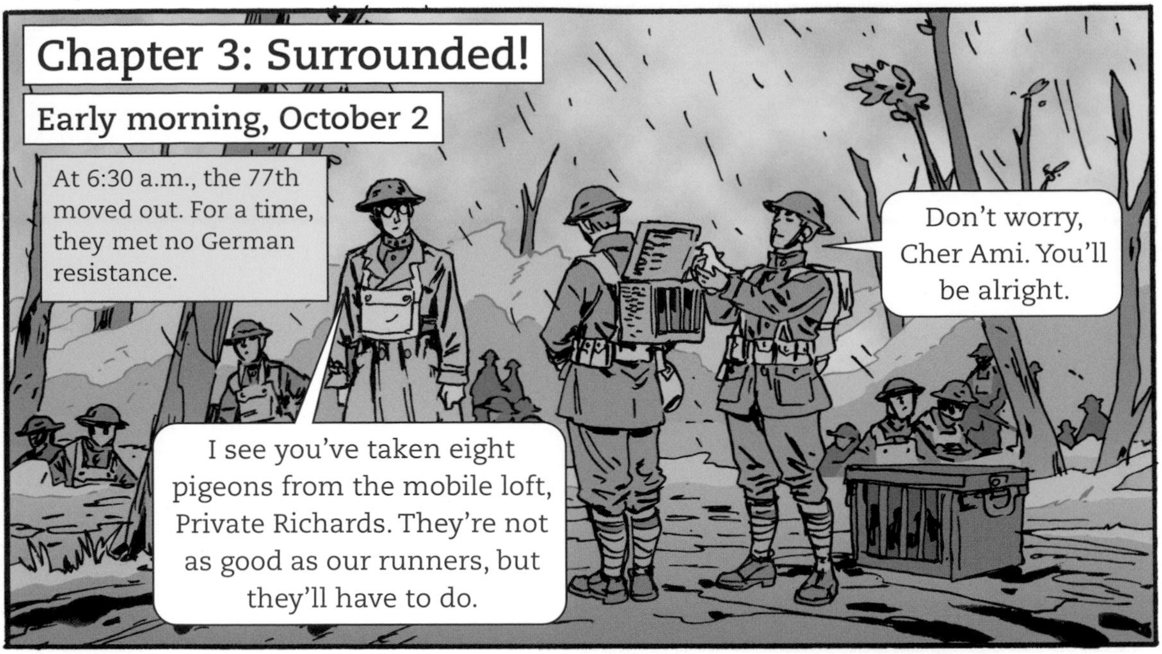
Chapter 3: Surrounded!
Early morning, October 2
At 6:30 a.m., the 77th moved out. For a time, they met no German resistance.
Don't worry, Cher Ami. You'll be alright.
I see you've taken eight pigeons from the mobile loft, Private Richards. They're not as good as our runners, but they'll have to do.

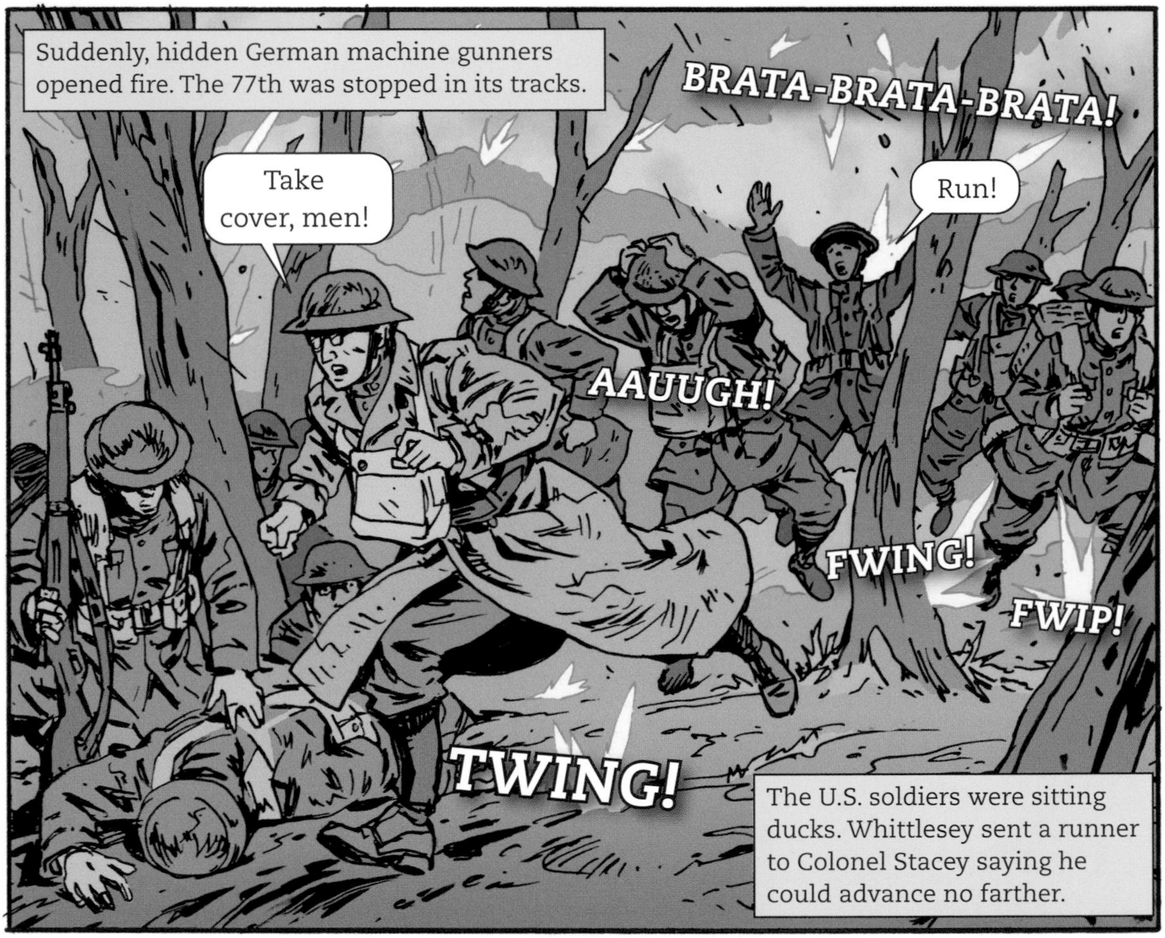
Suddenly, hidden German machine gunners opened fire. The 77th was stopped in its tracks.
BRATA-BRATA-BRATA!
Take cover, men!
Run!
AAUUGH!
FWING!
FWIP!
TWING!
The U.S. soldiers were sitting ducks. Whittlesey sent a runner to Colonel Stacey saying he could advance no farther.

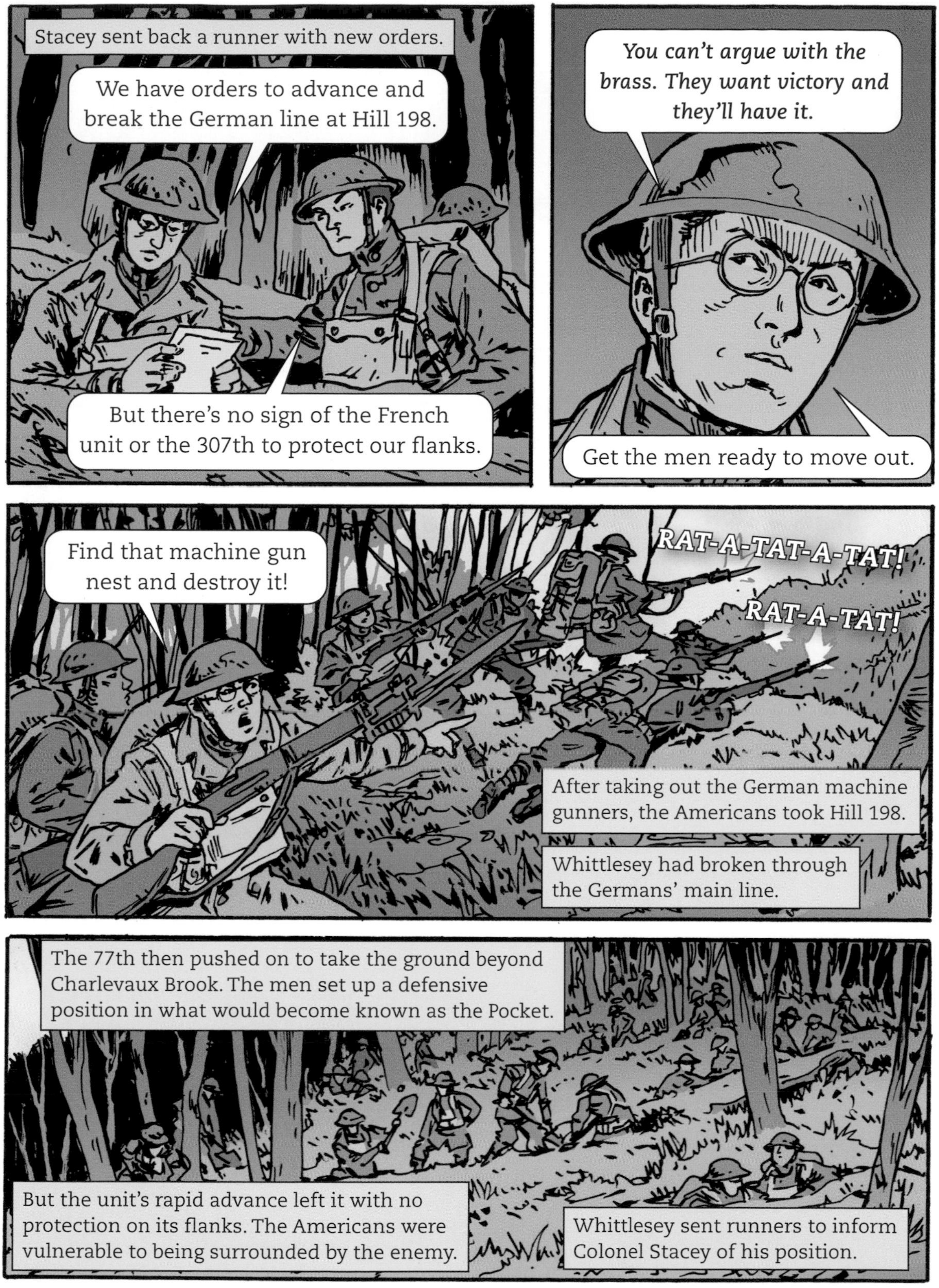
Stacey sent back a runner with new orders.
We have orders to advance and break the German line at Hill 198.
But there's no sign of the French unit or the 307th to protect our flanks.
You can't argue with the brass. They want victory and they'll have it.
Get the men ready to move out.
Find that machine gun nest and destroy it!
RAT-A-TAT-A-TAT!
RAT-A-TAT!
After taking out the German machine gunners, the Americans took Hill 198.
Whittlesey had broken through the Germans' main line.
The 77th then pushed on to take the ground beyond Charlevaux Brook. The men set up a defensive position in what would become known as the Pocket.
But the unit's rapid advance left it with no protection on its flanks. The Americans were vulnerable to being surrounded by the enemy.
Whittlesey sent runners to inform Colonel Stacey of his position.

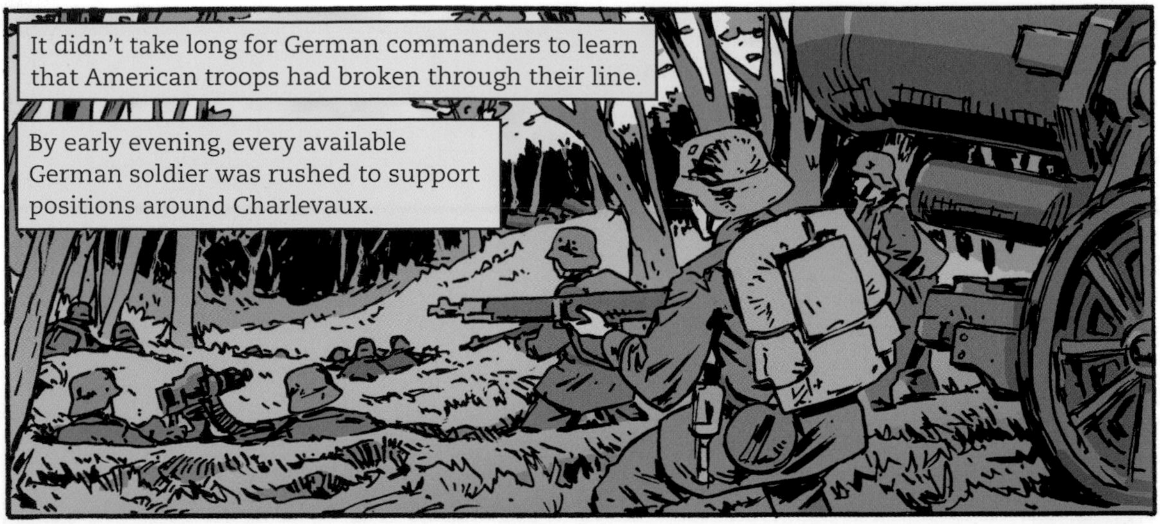
It didn't take long for German commanders to learn that American troops had broken through their line.
By early evening, every available German soldier was rushed to support positions around Charlevaux.

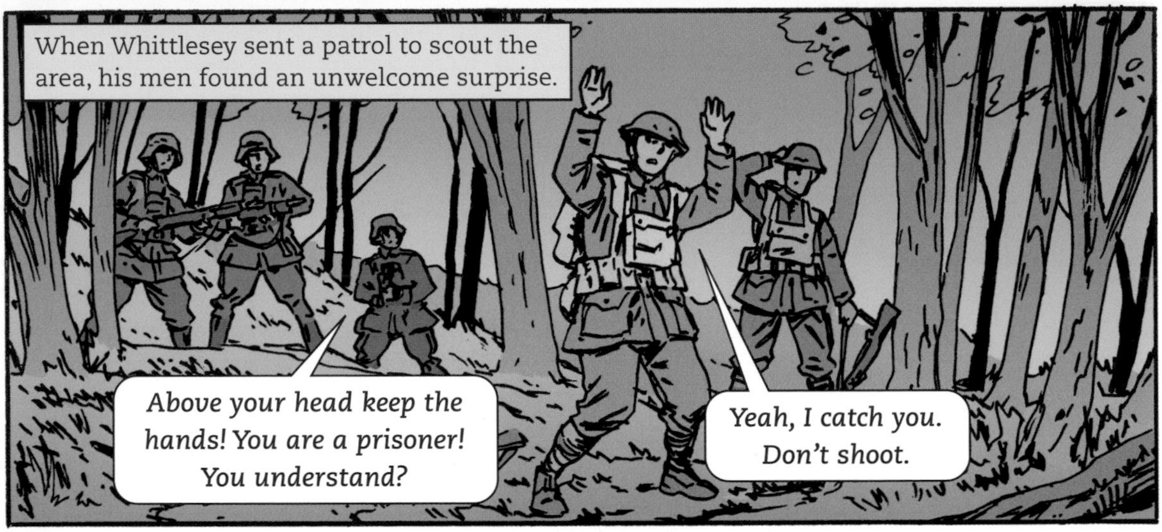
When Whittlesey sent a patrol to scout the area, his men found an unwelcome surprise.
Above your head keep the hands! You are a prisoner! You understand?
Yeah, I catch you. Don't shoot.

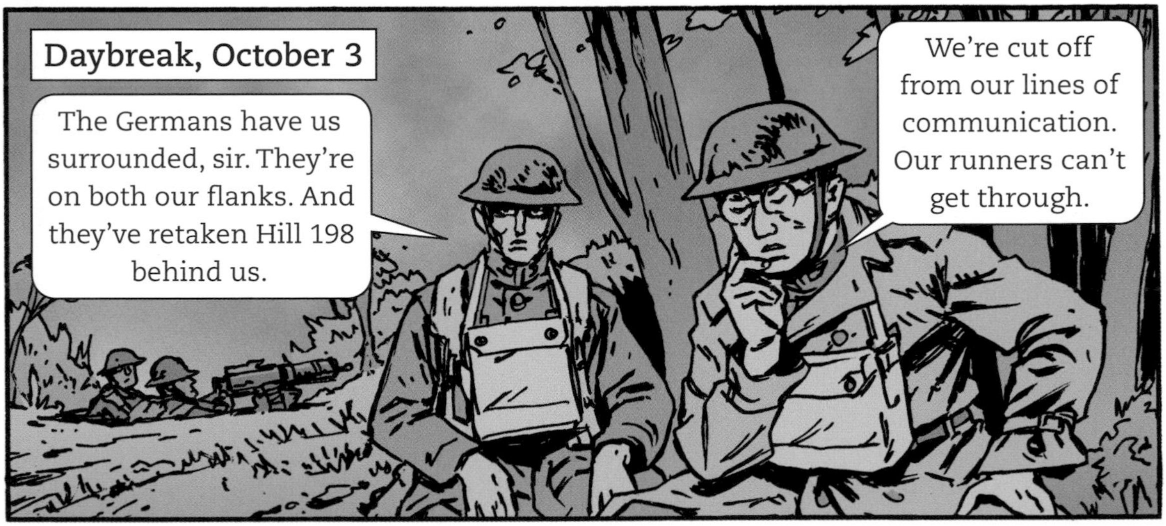
Daybreak, October 3
The Germans have us surrounded, sir. They're on both our flanks. And they've retaken Hill 198 behind us.
We're cut off from our lines of communication. Our runners can't get through.

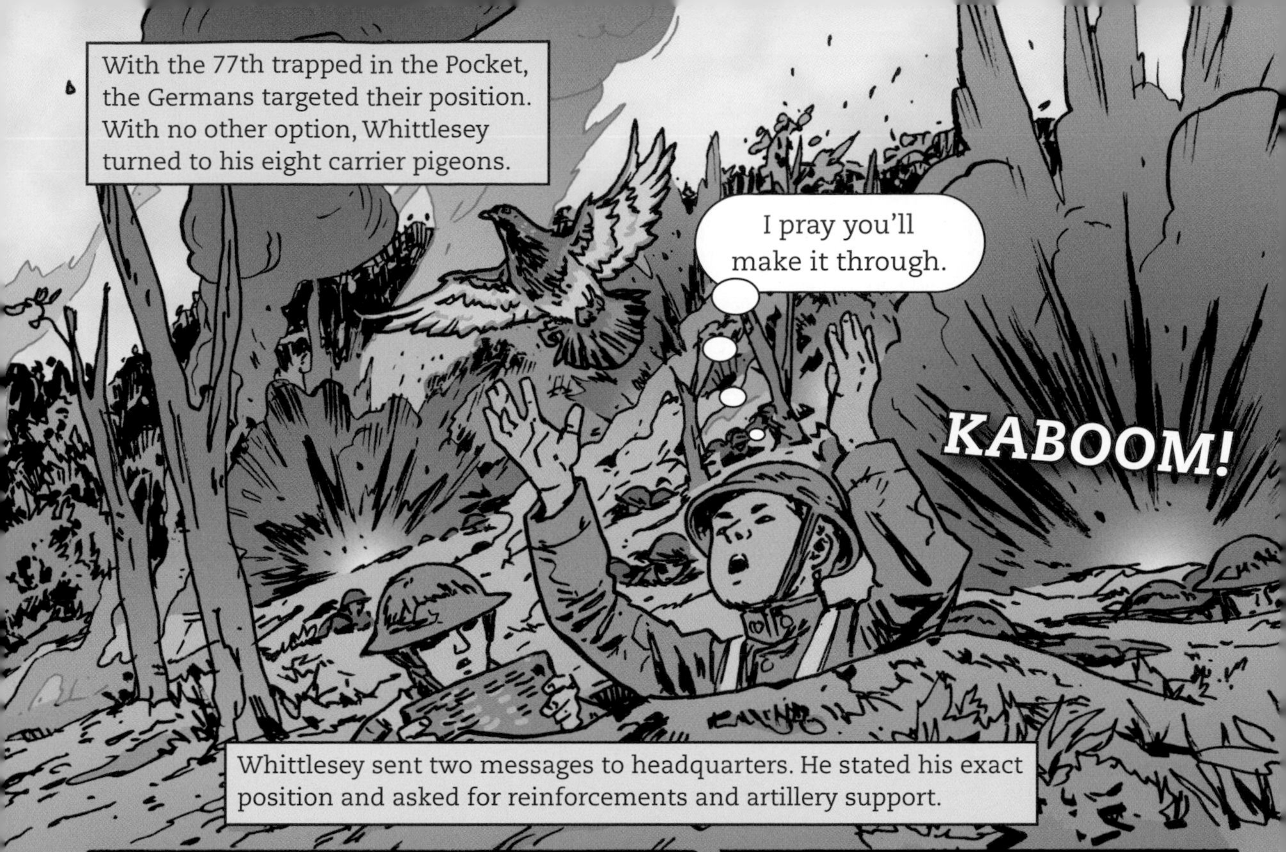
With the 77th trapped in the Pocket, the Germans targeted their position. With no other option, Whittlesey turned to his eight carrier pigeons.
I pray you'll make it through.
KABOOM!
Whittlesey sent two messages to headquarters. He stated his exact position and asked for reinforcements and artillery support.

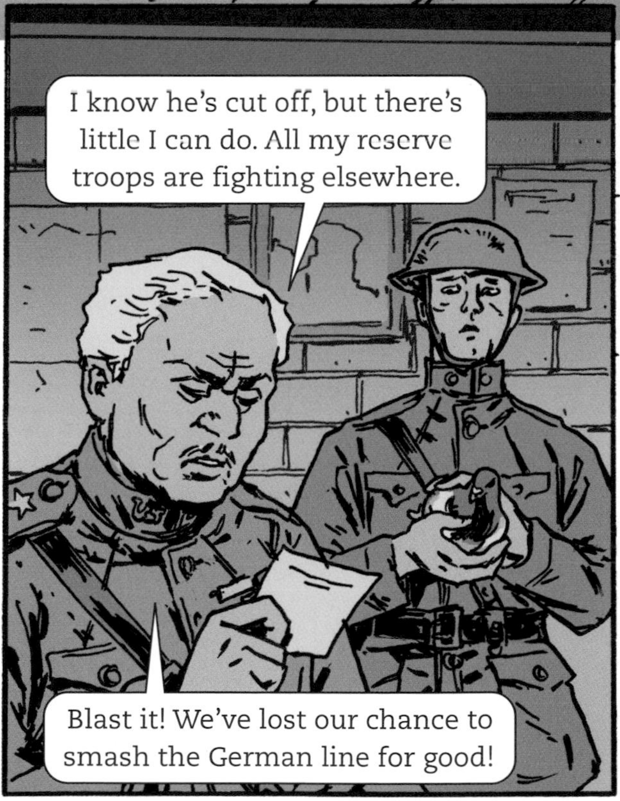
I know he's cut off, but there's little I can do. All my reserve troops are fighting elsewhere.
Blast it! We've lost our chance to smash the German line for good!

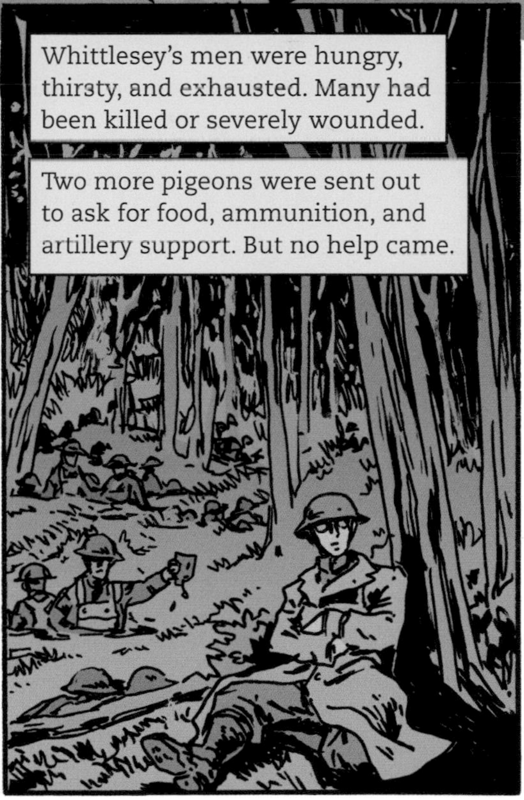
Whittlesey's men were hungry, thirsty, and exhausted. Many had been killed or severely wounded.
Two more pigeons were sent out to ask for food, ammunition, and artillery support. But no help came.

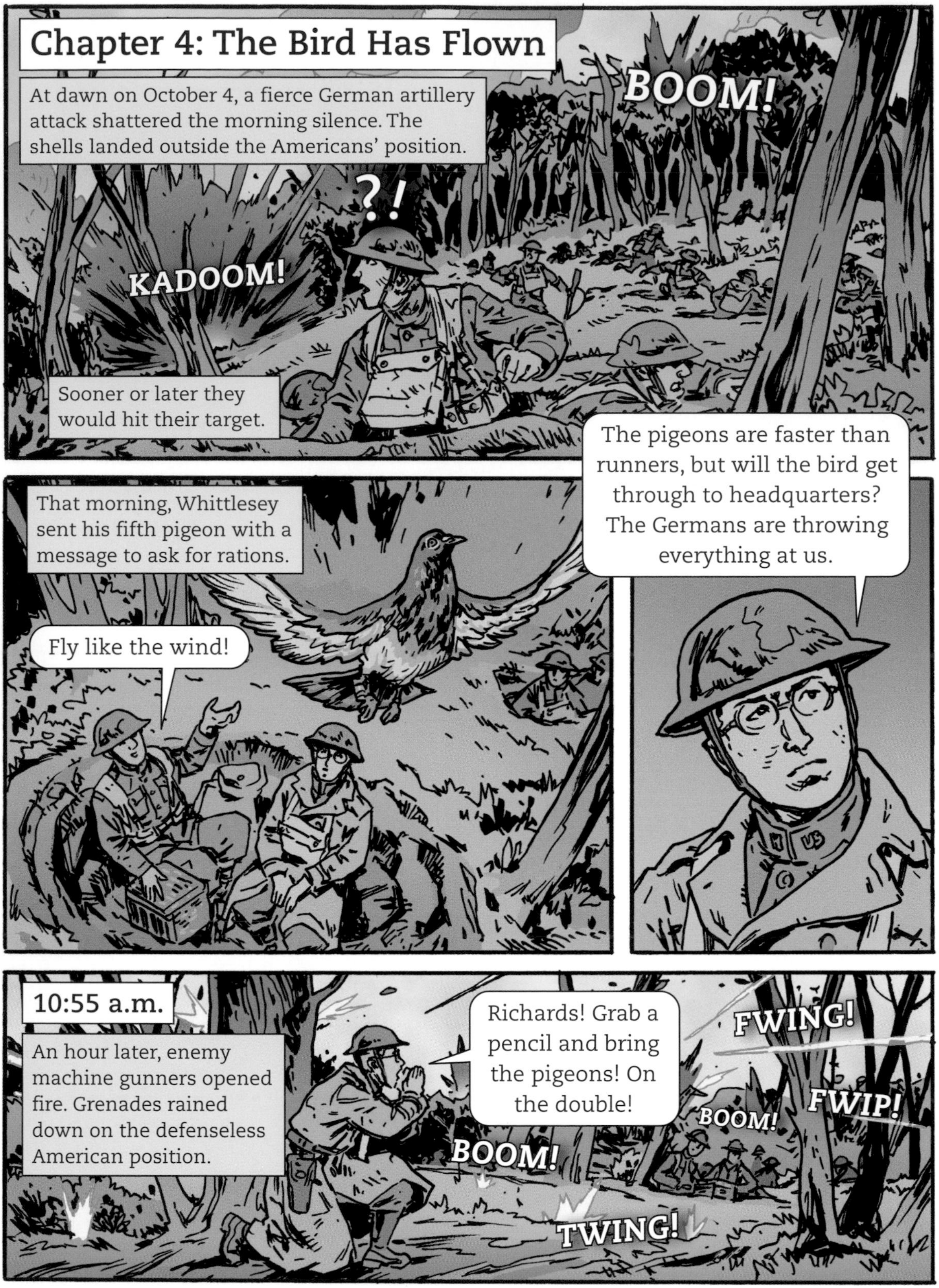
Chapter 4: The Bird Has Flown
At dawn on October 4, a fierce German artillery attack shattered the morning silence. The shells landed outside the Americans' position.
BOOM!
?!
KADOOM!
Sooner or later they would hit their target.
That morning, Whittlesey sent his fifth pigeon with a message to ask for rations.
Fly like the wind!
The pigeons are faster than runners, but will the bird get through to headquarters? The Germans are throwing everything at us.
10:55 a.m.
An hour later, enemy machine gunners opened fire. Grenades rained down on the defenseless American position.
Richards! Grab a pencil and bring the pigeons! On the double!
FWING!
FWIP!
BOOM!
BOOM!
TWING!

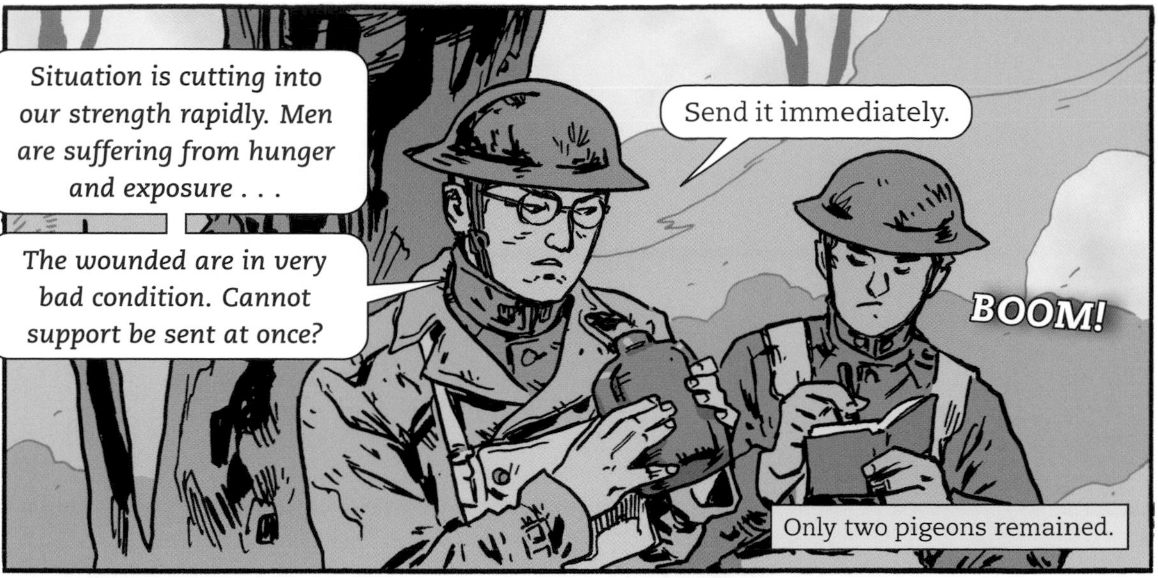
Situation is cutting into our strength rapidly. Men are suffering from hunger and exposure . . .
The wounded are in very bad condition. Cannot support be sent at once?
Send it immediately.
BOOM!
Only two pigeons remained.

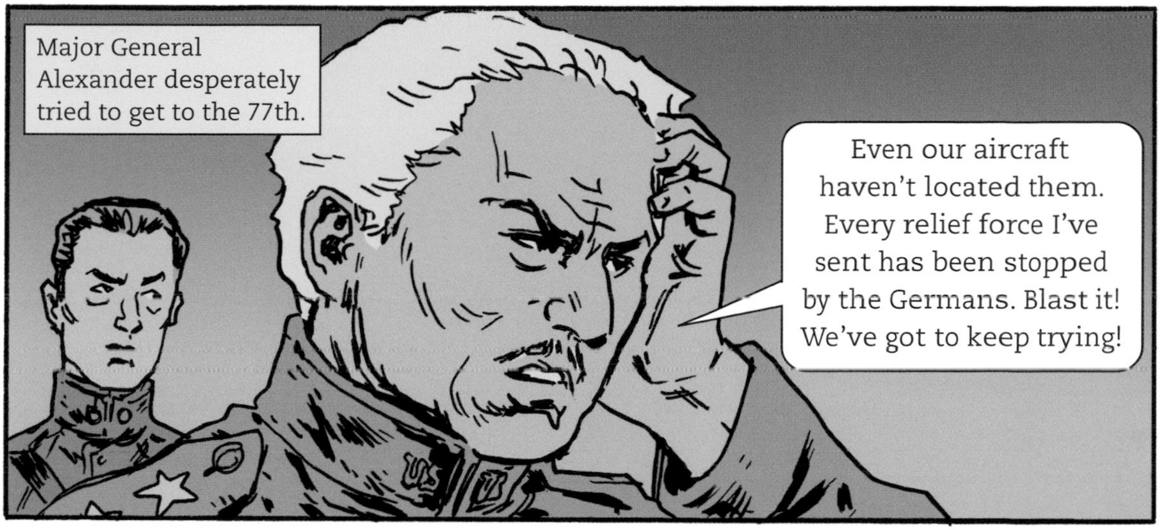
Major General Alexander desperately tried to get to the 77th.
Even our aircraft haven't located them. Every relief force I've sent has been stopped by the Germans. Blast it! We've got to keep trying!

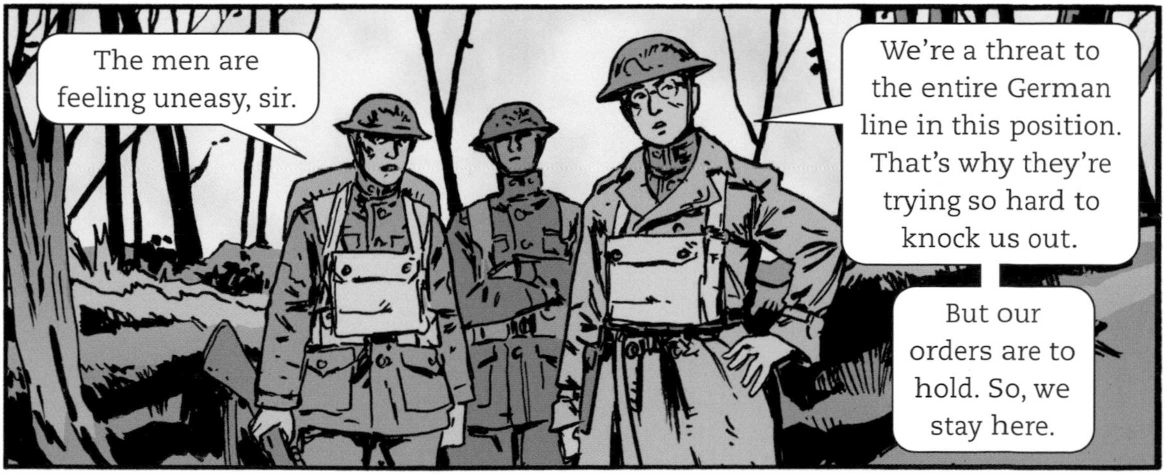
The men are feeling uneasy, sir.
We're a threat to the entire German line in this position. That's why they're trying so hard to knock us out.
But our orders are to hold. So, we stay here.

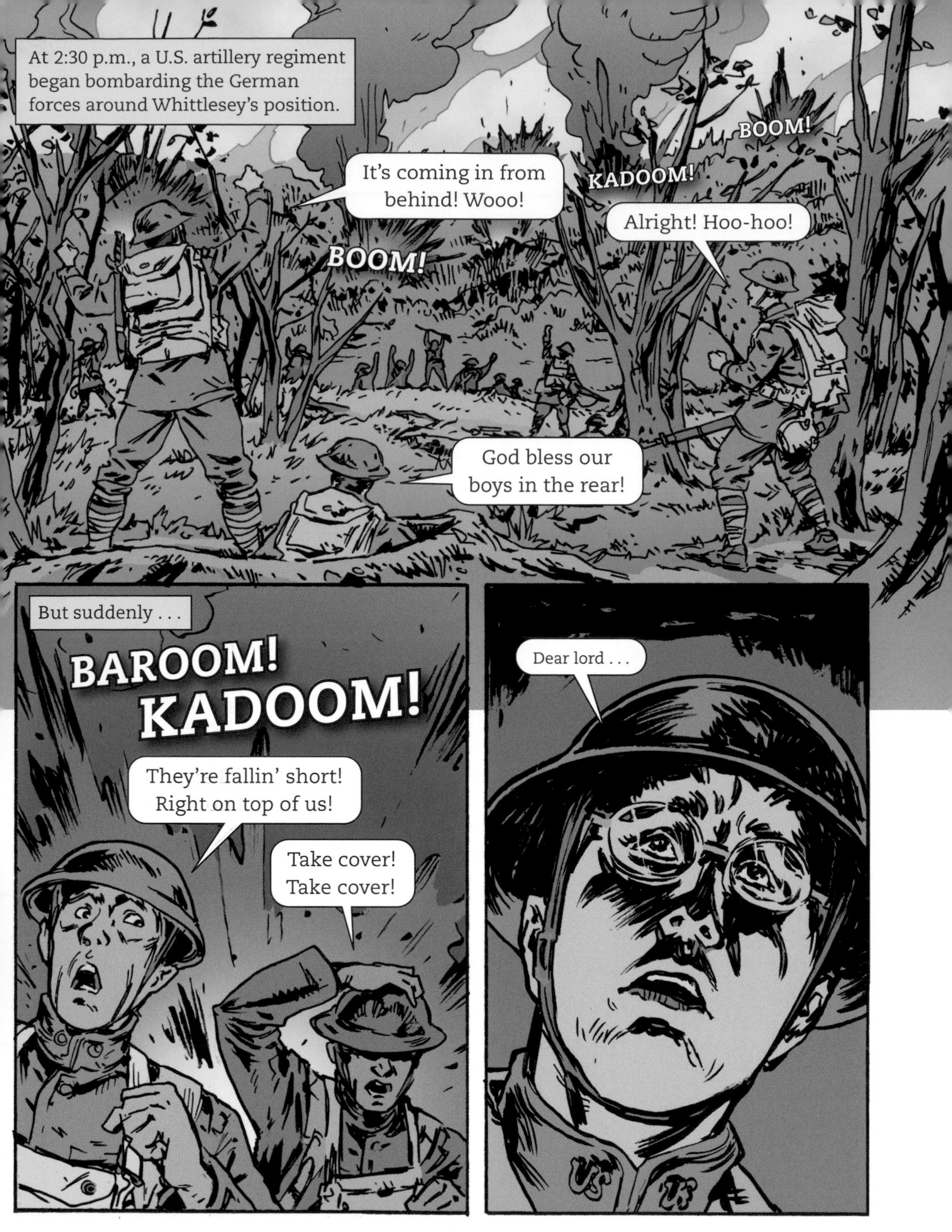

At 2:30 p.m., a U.S. artillery regiment began bombarding the German forces around Whittlesey's position.
It's coming in from behind! Wooo!
BOOM!
KADOOM!
BOOM!
Alright! Hoo-hoo!
God bless our boys in the rear!
But suddenly . . .
BAROOM!
KADOOM!
They're fallin' short! Right on top of us!
Take cover! Take cover!
Dear lord . . .

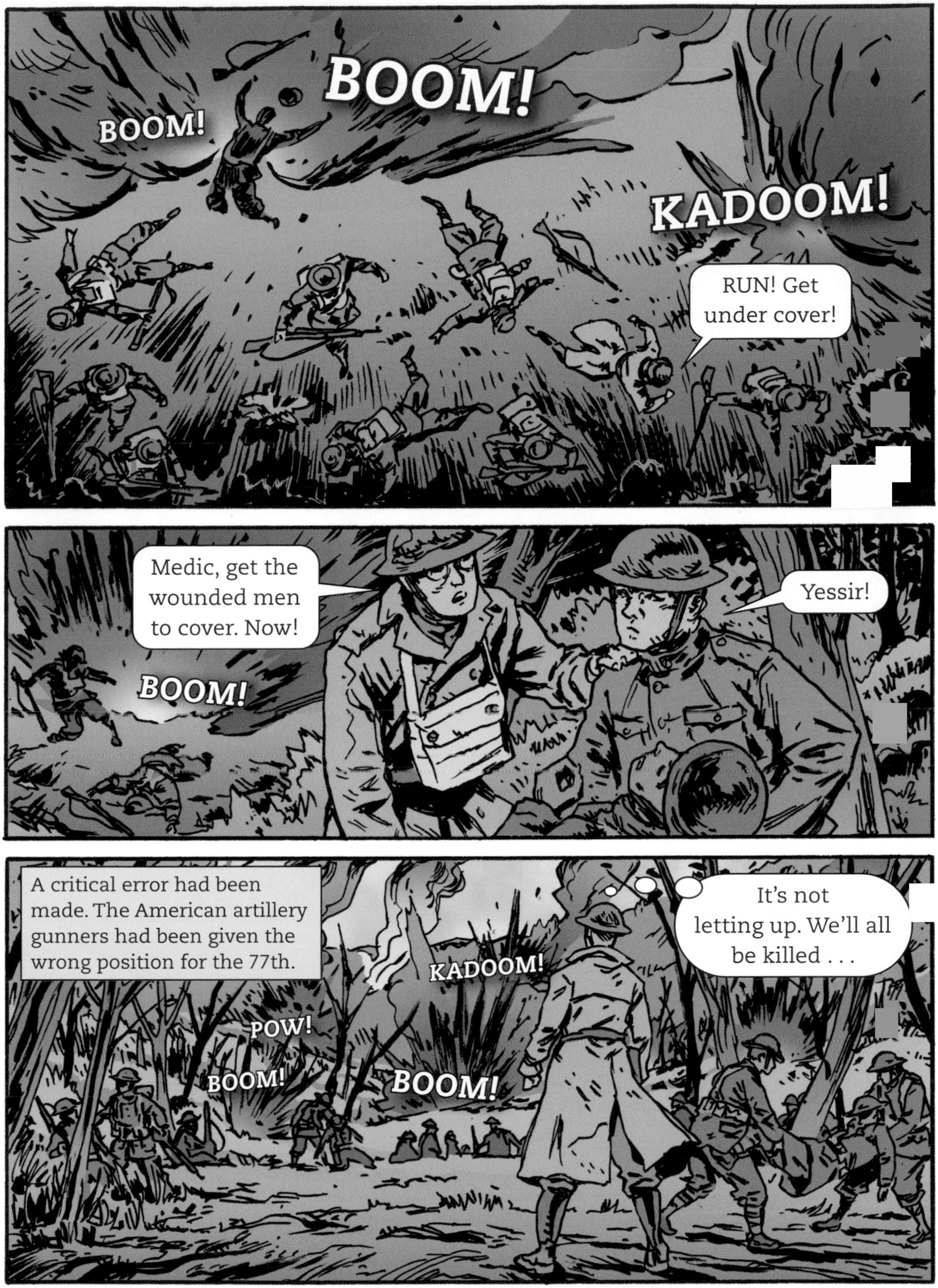
BOOM!
BOOM!
KADOOM!
RUN! Get under cover!
Medic, get the wounded men to cover. Now!
Yessir!
BOOM!
A critical error had been made. The American artillery gunners had been given the wrong position for the 77th.
It's not letting up. We'll all be killed . . .
KADOOM!
POW!
BOOM!
BOOM!

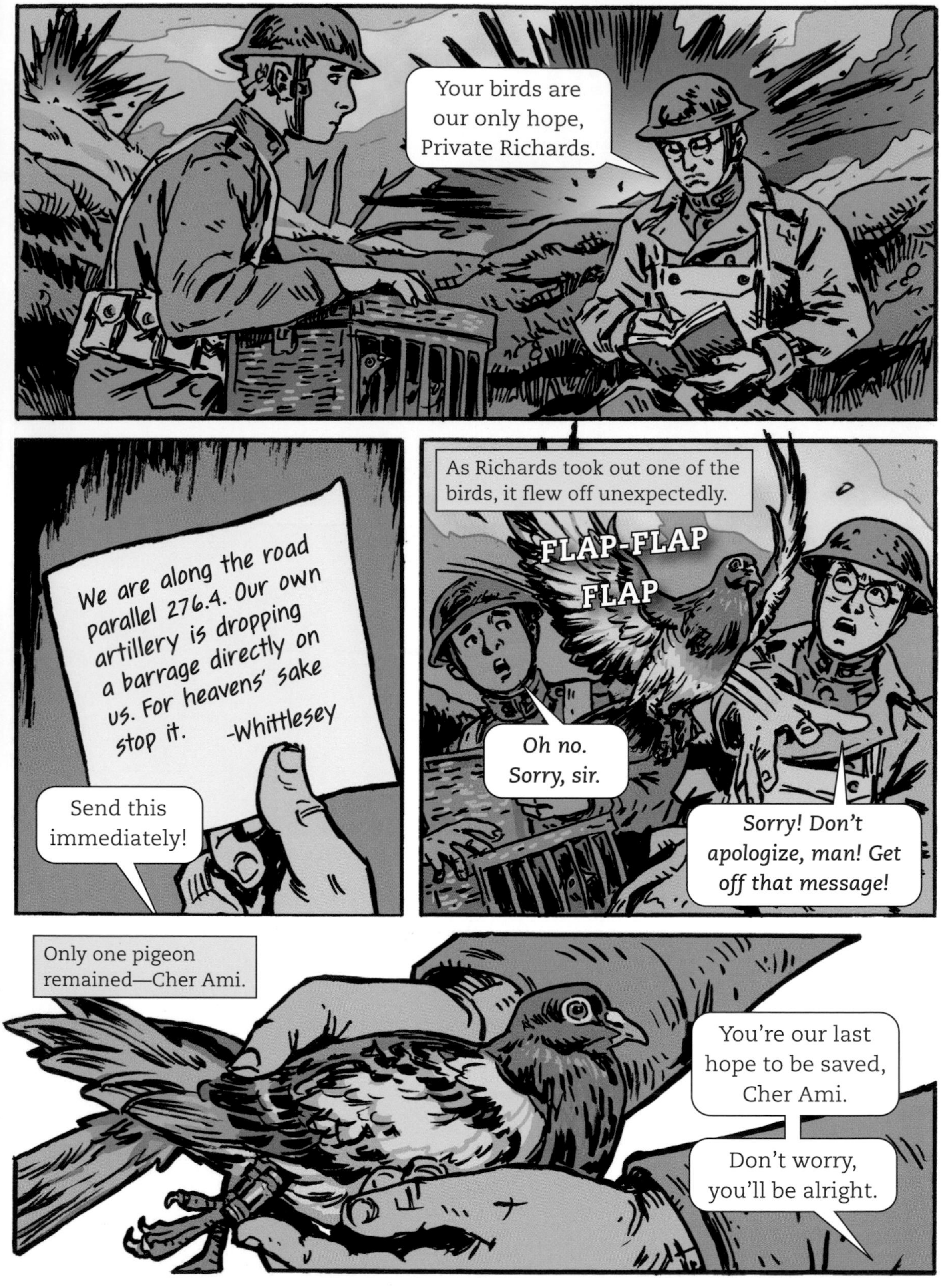
Your birds are our only hope, Private Richards.
We are along the road parallel 276.4. Our own artillery is dropping a barrage directly on us. For heavens' sake stop it. -Whittlesey
Send this immediately!
As Richards took out one of the birds, it flew off unexpectedly.
FLAP-FLAP
FLAP
Oh no. Sorry, sir.
Sorry! Don't apologize, man! Get off that message!
Only one pigeon remained—Cher Ami.
You're our last hope to be saved, Cher Ami.
Don't worry, you'll be alright.

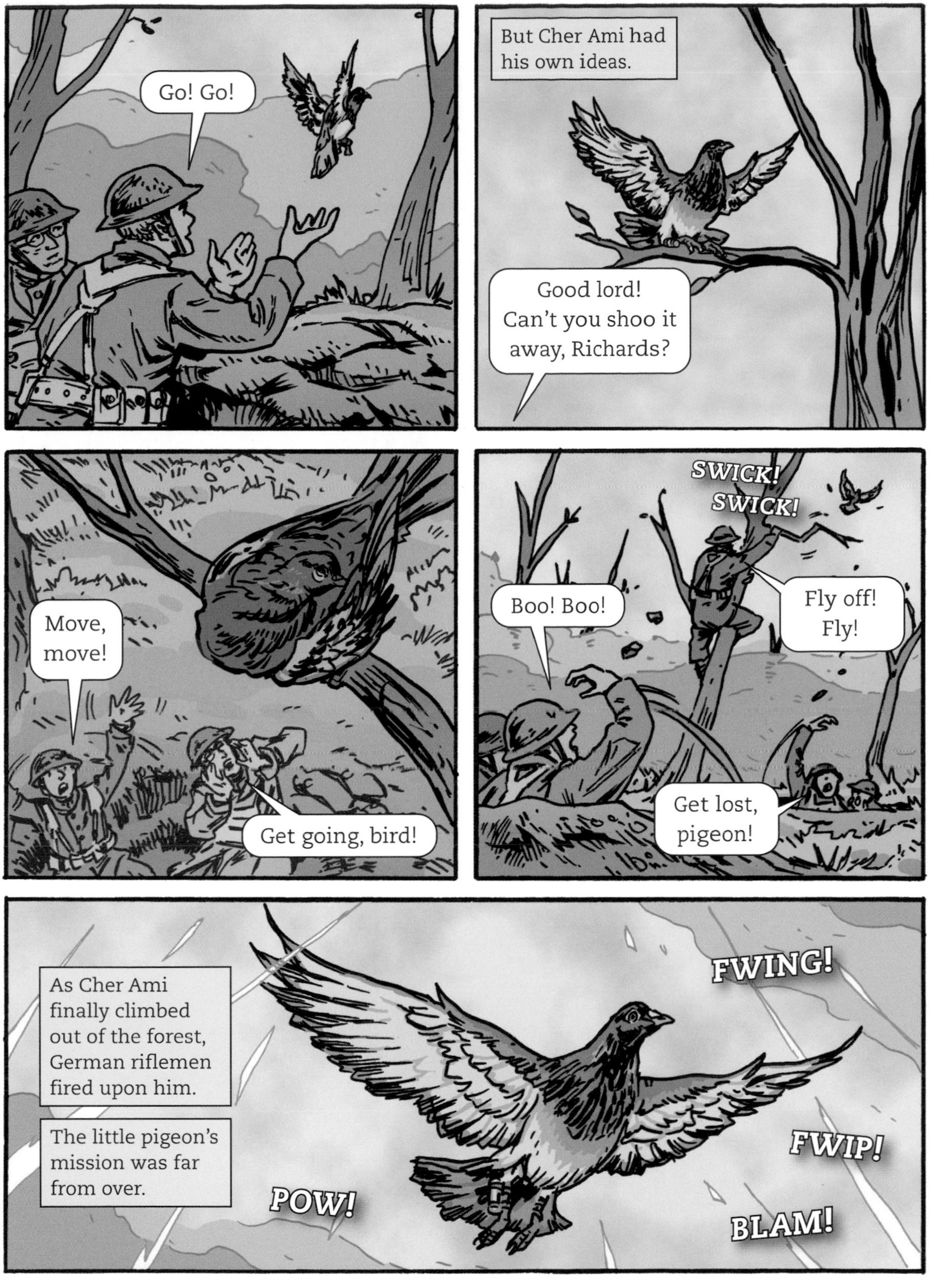
Go! Go!
But Cher Ami had his own ideas.
Good lord! Can't you shoo it away, Richards?
Move, move!
Get going, bird!
SWICK! SWICK!
Boo! Boo!
Fly off! Fly!
Get lost, pigeon!
As Cher Ami finally climbed out of the forest, German riflemen fired upon him.
The little pigeon's mission was far from over.
FWING!
FWIP!
POW!
BLAM!

Chapter 5: World War I Savior Pigeon

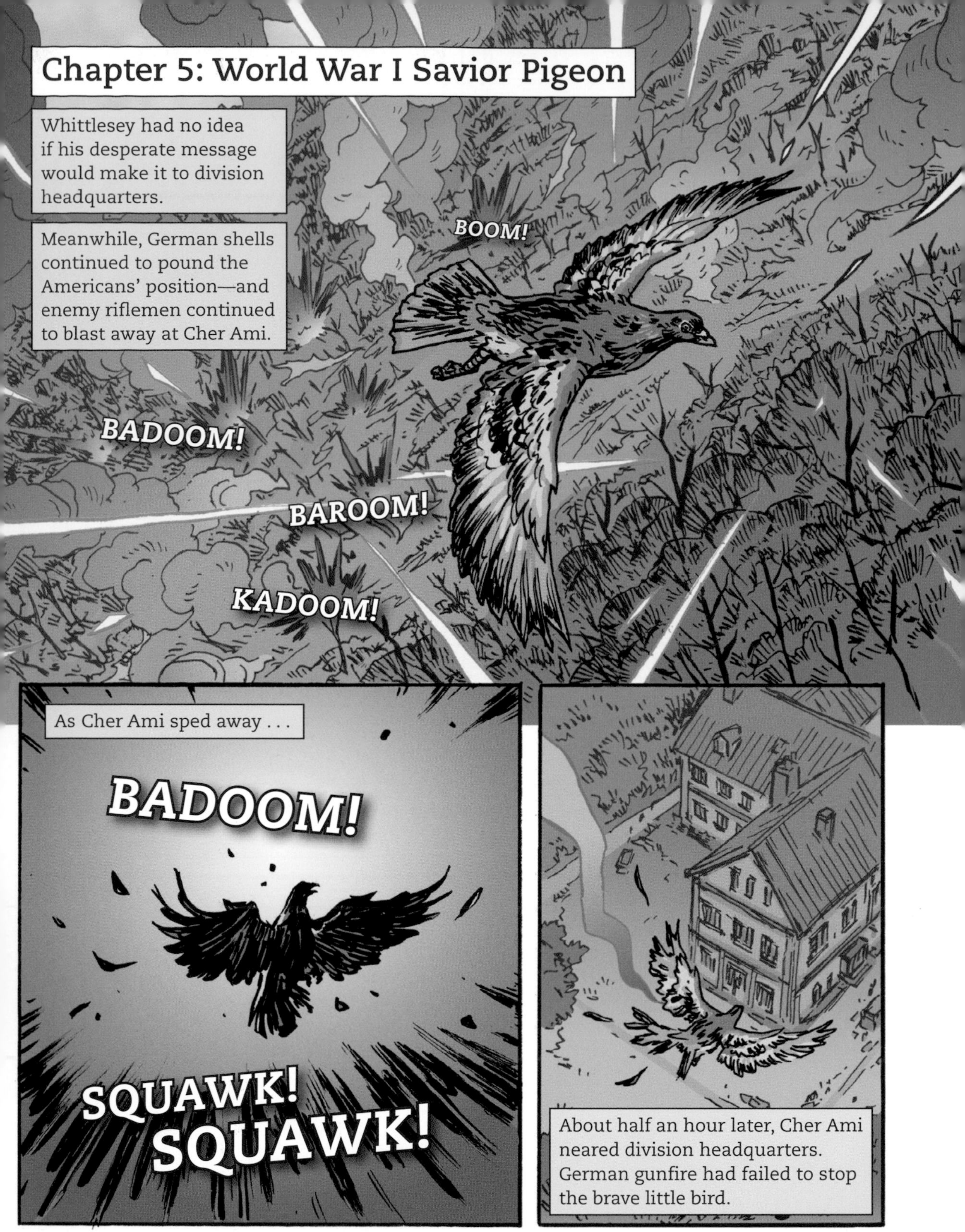

Whittlesey had no idea if his desperate message would make it to division headquarters.
Meanwhile, German shells continued to pound the Americans' position—and enemy riflemen continued to blast away at Cher Ami.
BOOM!
BADOOM!
BAROOM!
KADOOM!
As Cher Ami sped away . . .
BADOOM!
SQUAWK!
SQUAWK!
About half an hour later, Cher Ami neared division headquarters. German gunfire had failed to stop the brave little bird.

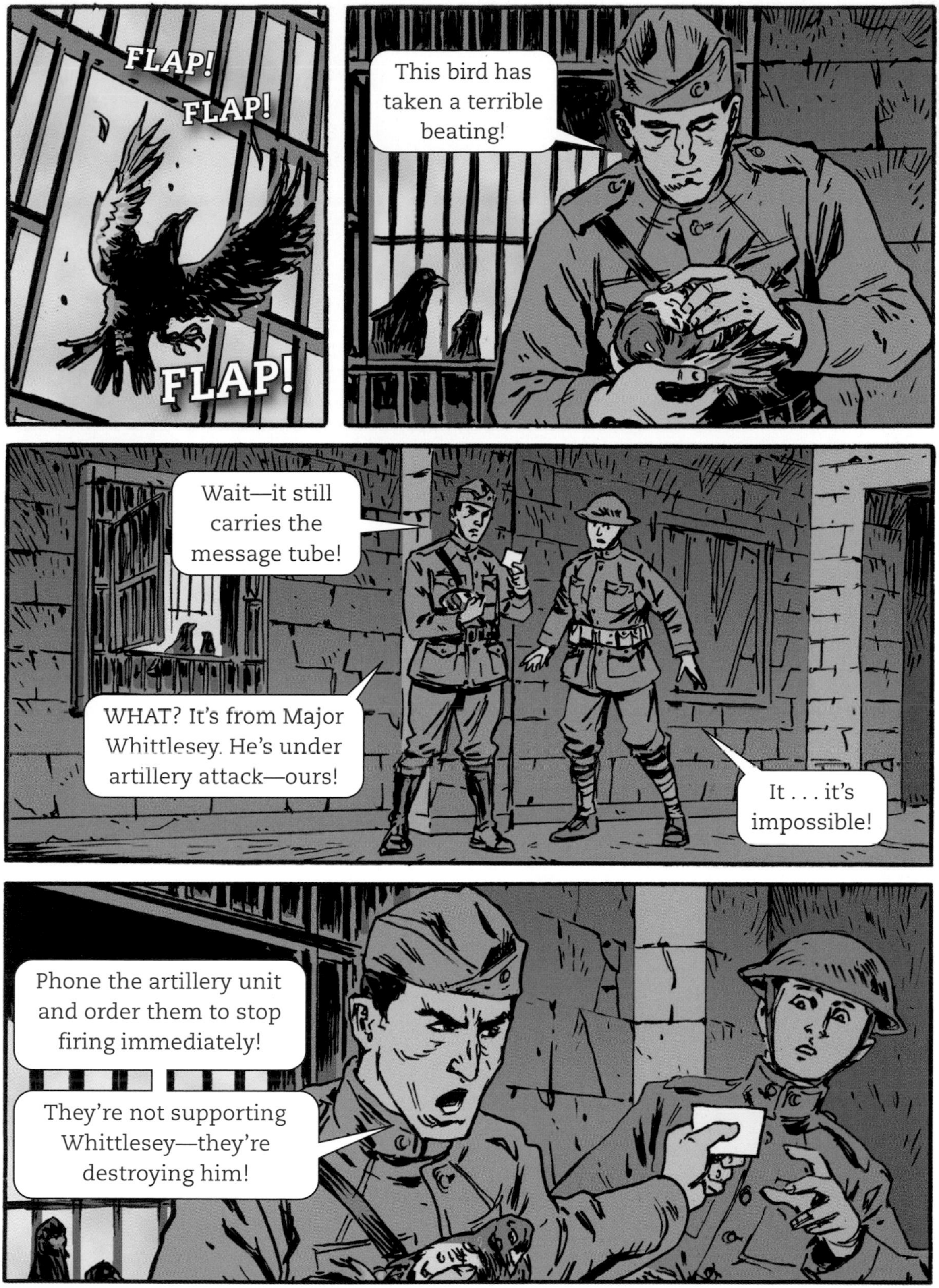
FLAP!
FLAP!
FLAP!
This bird has taken a terrible beating!
Wait—it still carries the message tube!
WHAT? It's from Major Whittlesey. He's under artillery attack—ours!
It . . . it's impossible!
Phone the artillery unit and order them to stop firing immediately!
They're not supporting Whittlesey—they're destroying him!

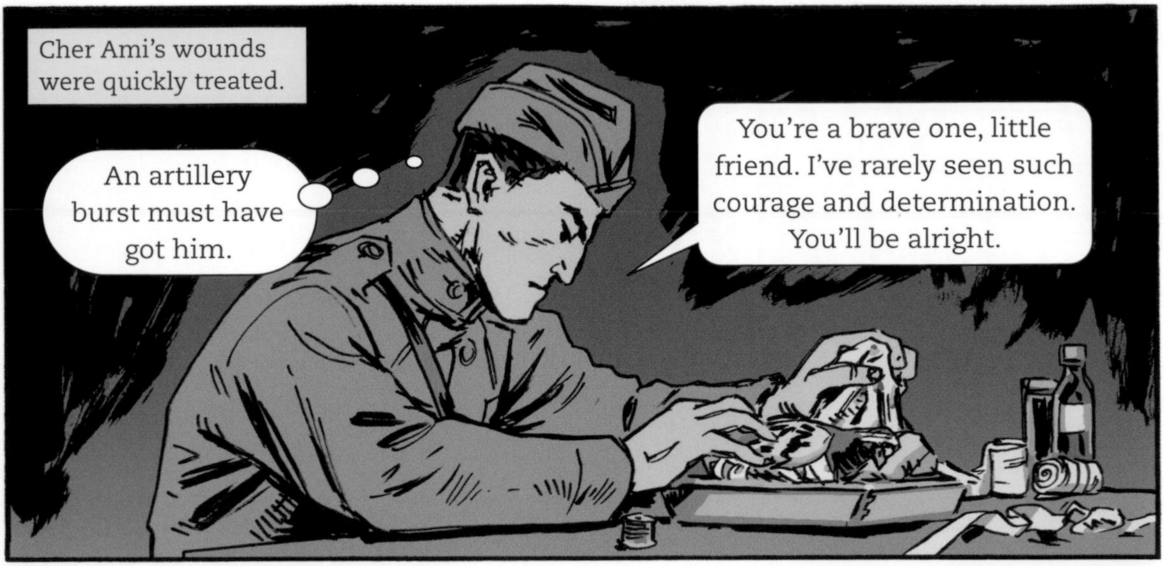
Cher Ami's wounds were quickly treated.
An artillery burst must have got him.
You're a brave one, little friend. I've rarely seen such courage and determination. You'll be alright.

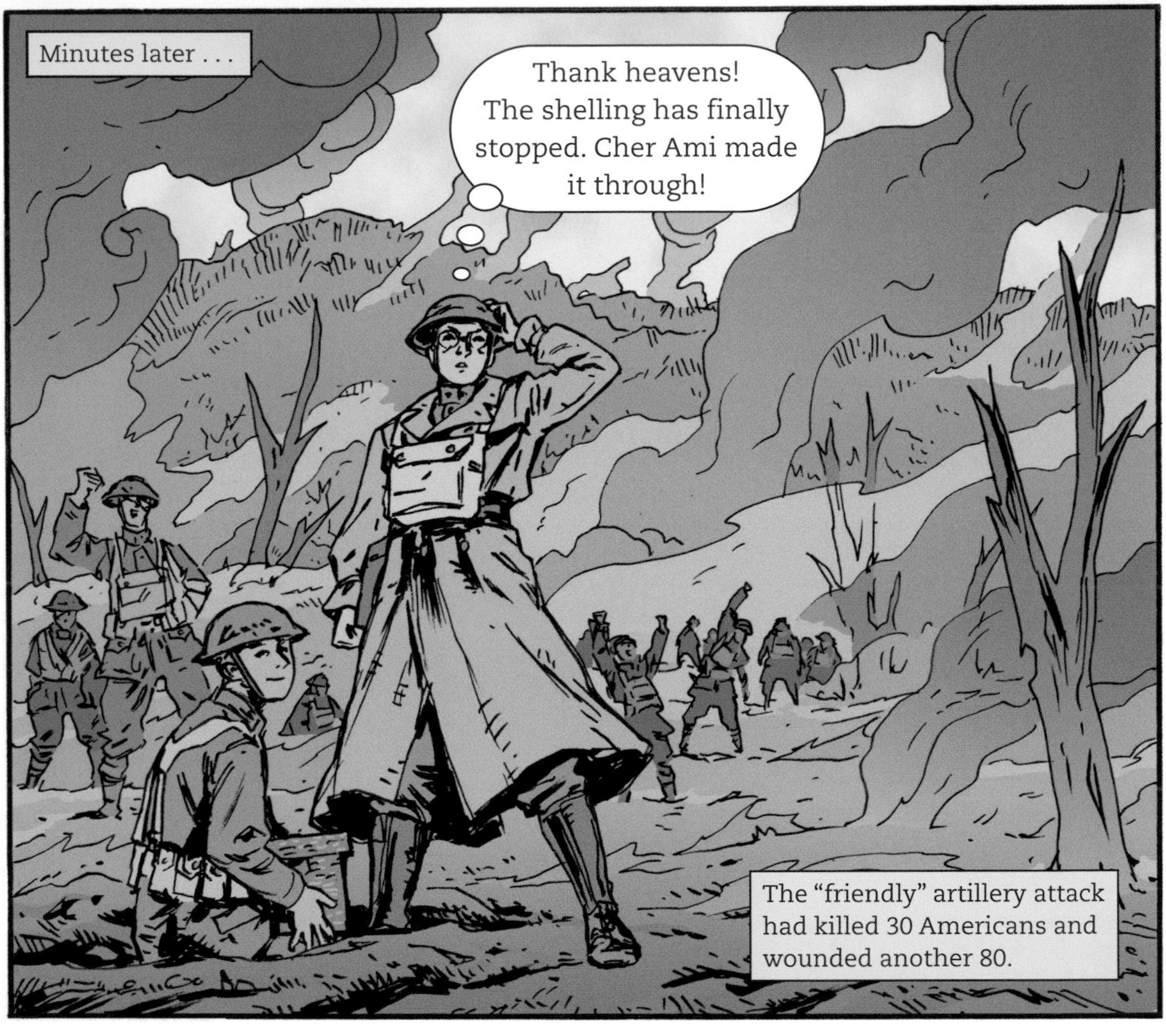
Minutes later . . .
Thank heavens! The shelling has finally stopped. Cher Ami made it through!
The "friendly" artillery attack had killed 30 Americans and wounded another 80.

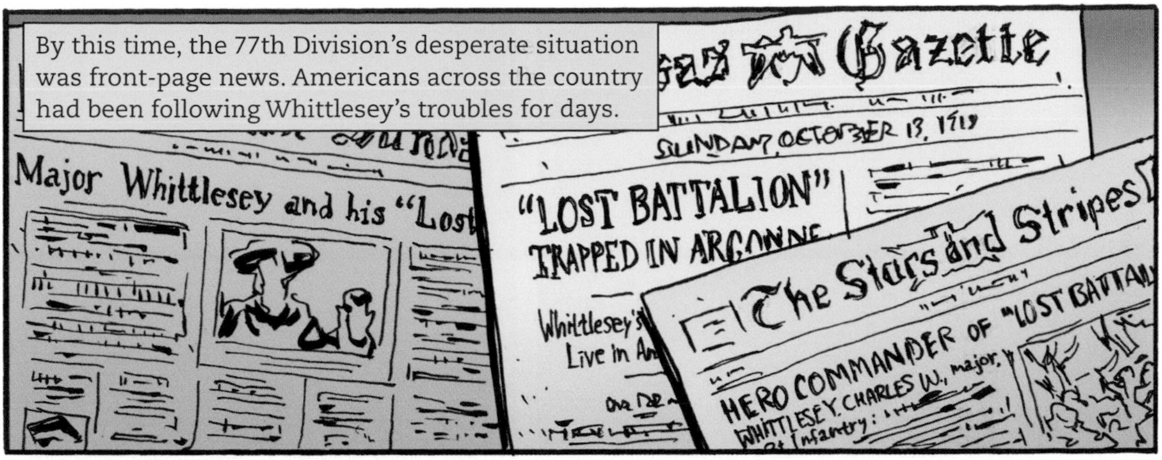
By this time, the 77th Division's desperate situation was front-page news. Americans across the country had been following Whittlesey's troubles for days.
Gazette
Major Whittlesey and his "Lost
"LOST BATTALION"
TRAPPED IN ARGONNE
The Stars and Stripes
HERO COMMANDER OF "LOST BATTA
WHITTLESEY, CHARLES W., major,

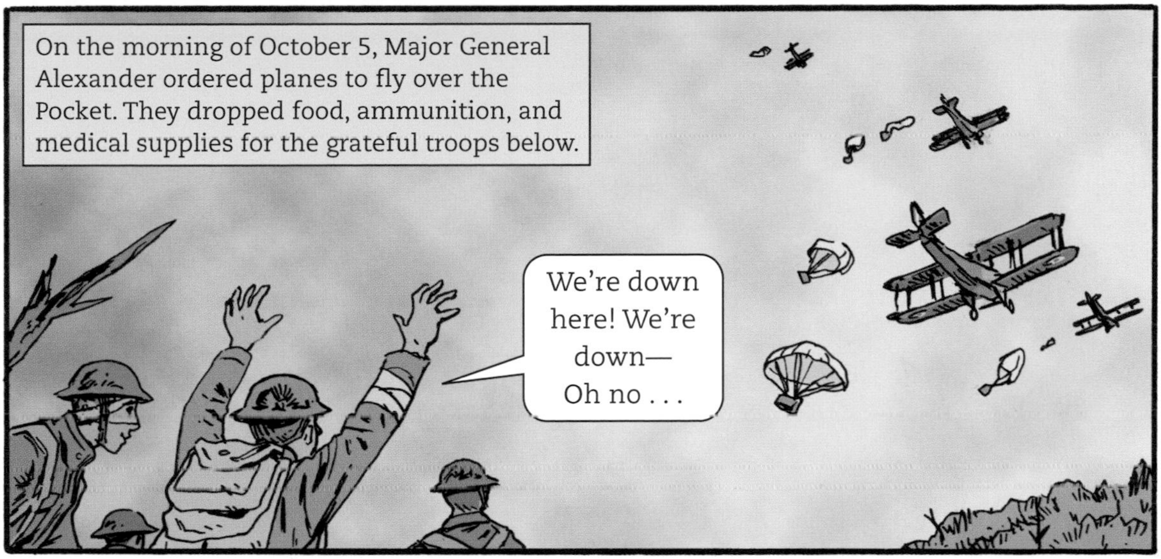
On the morning of October 5, Major General Alexander ordered planes to fly over the Pocket. They dropped food, ammunition, and medical supplies for the grateful troops below.
We're down here! We're down— Oh no . . .

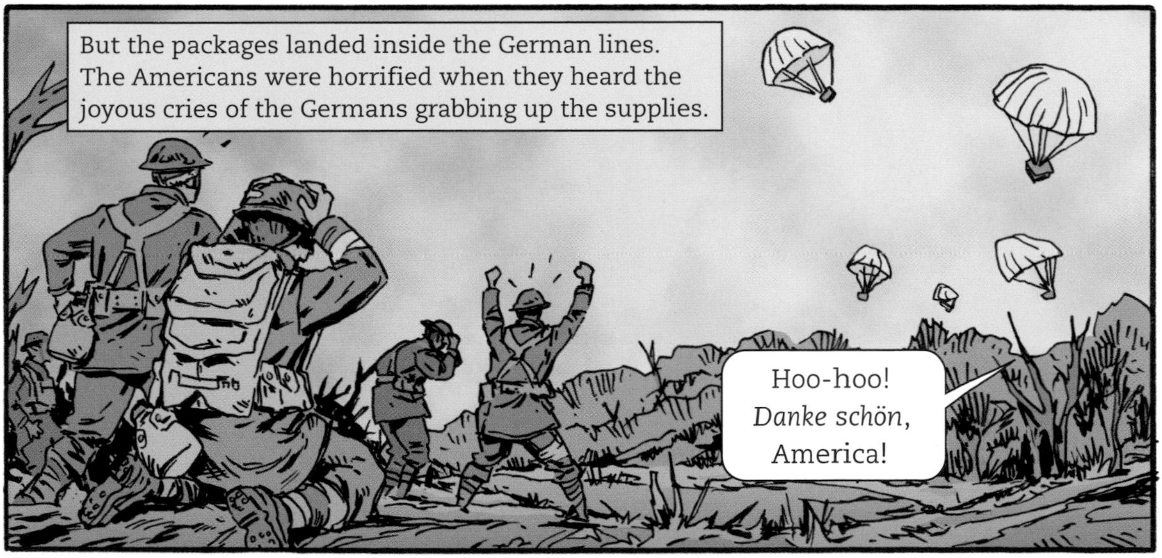
But the packages landed inside the German lines. The Americans were horrified when they heard the joyous cries of the Germans grabbing up the supplies.
Hoo-hoo! *Danke schön*, America!

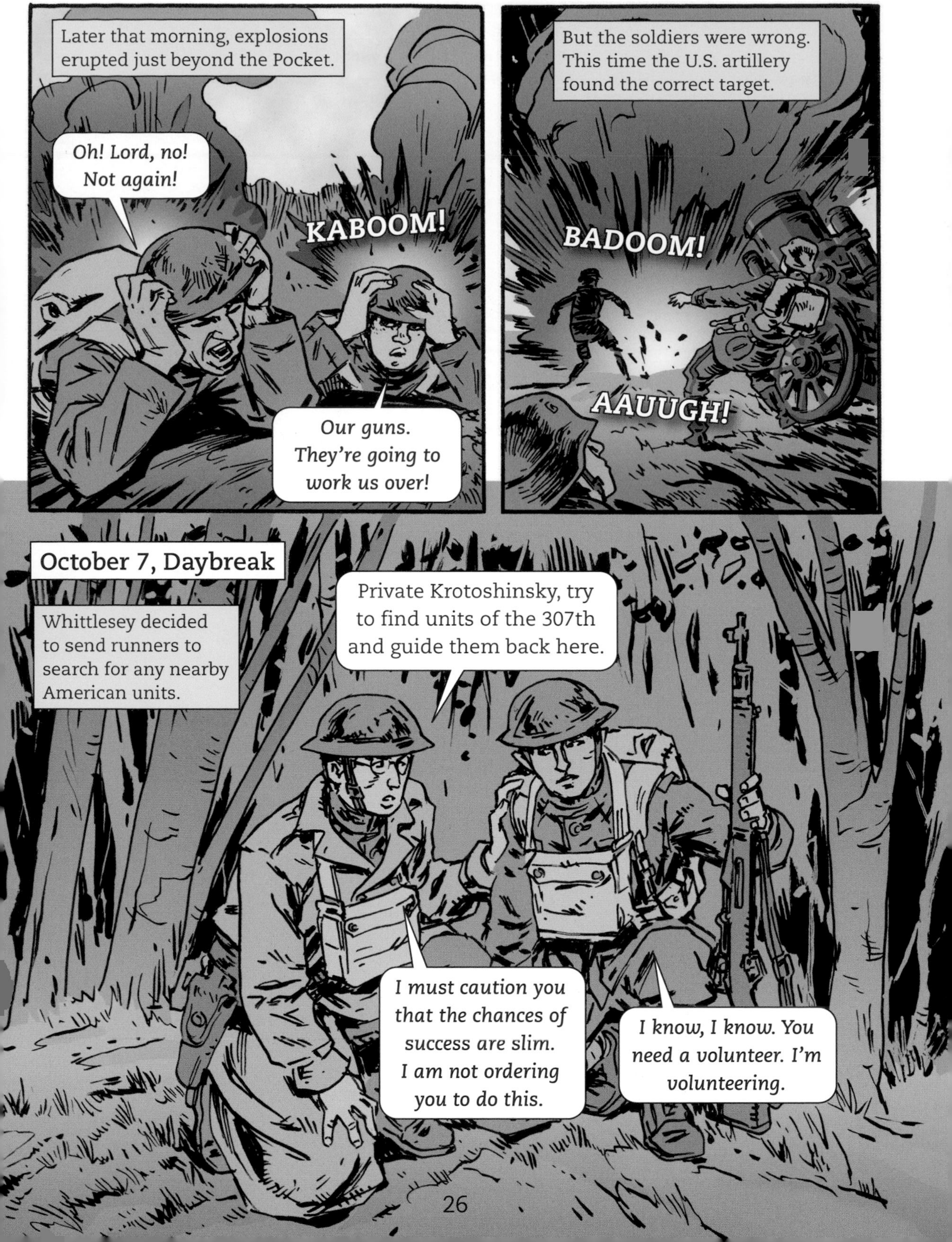
Later that morning, explosions erupted just beyond the Pocket.
Oh! Lord, no! Not again!
KABOOM!
Our guns. They're going to work us over!
But the soldiers were wrong. This time the U.S. artillery found the correct target.
BADOOM!
AAUUGH!
October 7, Daybreak
Whittlesey decided to send runners to search for any nearby American units.
Private Krotoshinsky, try to find units of the 307th and guide them back here.
I must caution you that the chances of success are slim. I am not ordering you to do this.
I know, I know. You need a volunteer. I'm volunteering.

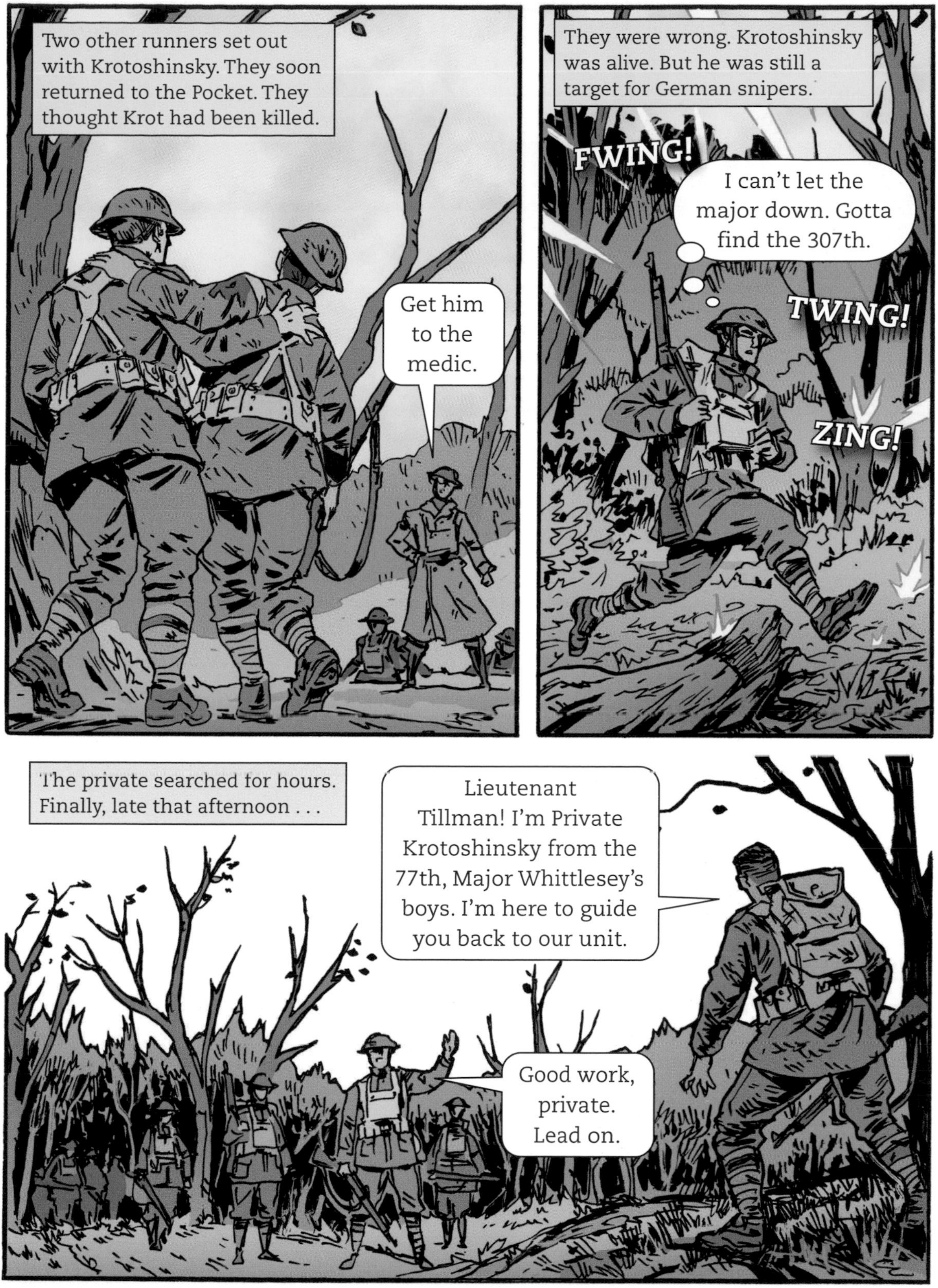
Two other runners set out with Krotoshinsky. They soon returned to the Pocket. They thought Krot had been killed.
Get him to the medic.
They were wrong. Krotoshinsky was alive. But he was still a target for German snipers.
FWING!
I can't let the major down. Gotta find the 307th.
TWING!
ZING!
The private searched for hours. Finally, late that afternoon . . .
Lieutenant Tillman! I'm Private Krotoshinsky from the 77th, Major Whittlesey's boys. I'm here to guide you back to our unit.
Good work, private. Lead on.

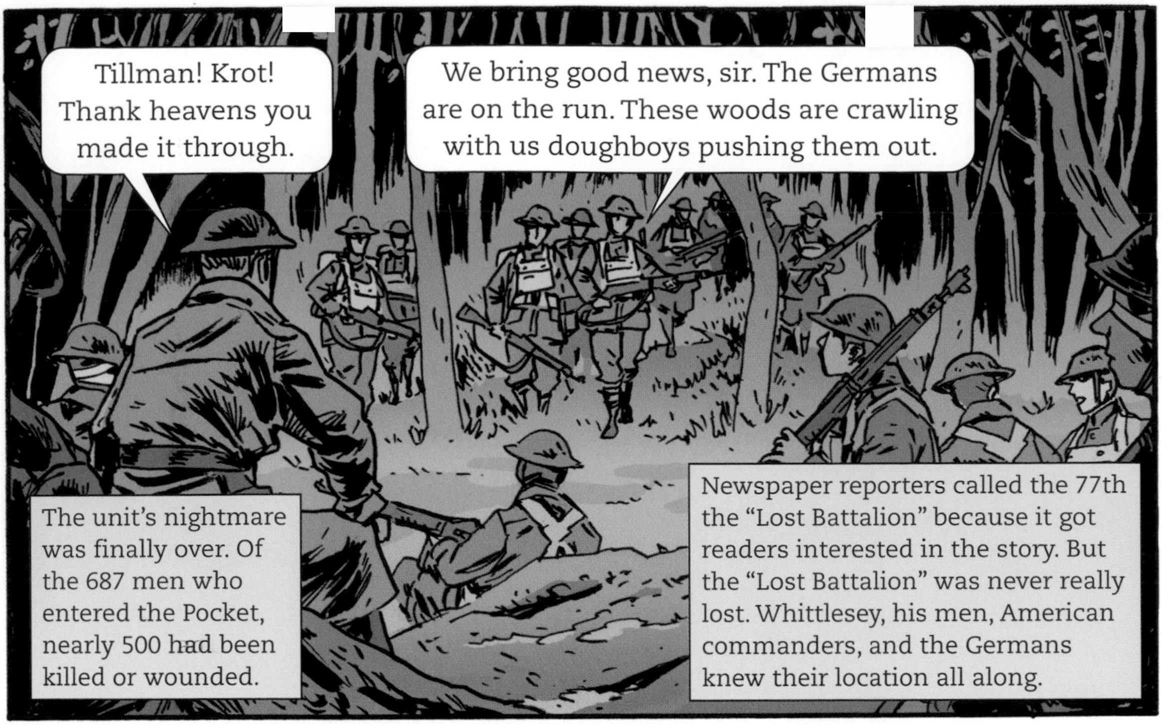

Tillman! Krot! Thank heavens you made it through.
We bring good news, sir. The Germans are on the run. These woods are crawling with us doughboys pushing them out.
The unit's nightmare was finally over. Of the 687 men who entered the Pocket, nearly 500 had been killed or wounded.
Newspaper reporters called the 77th the "Lost Battalion" because it got readers interested in the story. But the "Lost Battalion" was never really lost. Whittlesey, his men, American commanders, and the Germans knew their location all along.

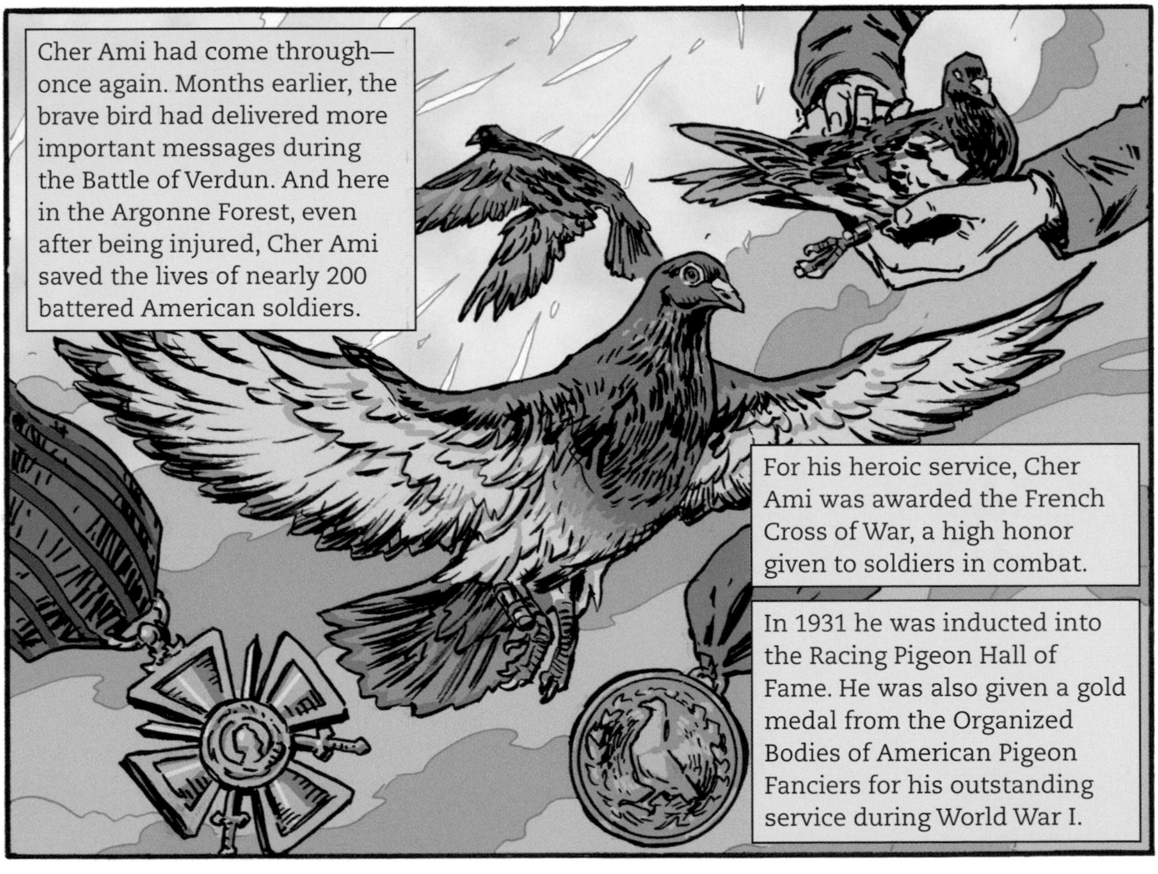

Cher Ami had come through—once again. Months earlier, the brave bird had delivered more important messages during the Battle of Verdun. And here in the Argonne Forest, even after being injured, Cher Ami saved the lives of nearly 200 battered American soldiers.
For his heroic service, Cher Ami was awarded the French Cross of War, a high honor given to soldiers in combat.
In 1931 he was inducted into the Racing Pigeon Hall of Fame. He was also given a gold medal from the Organized Bodies of American Pigeon Fanciers for his outstanding service during World War I.

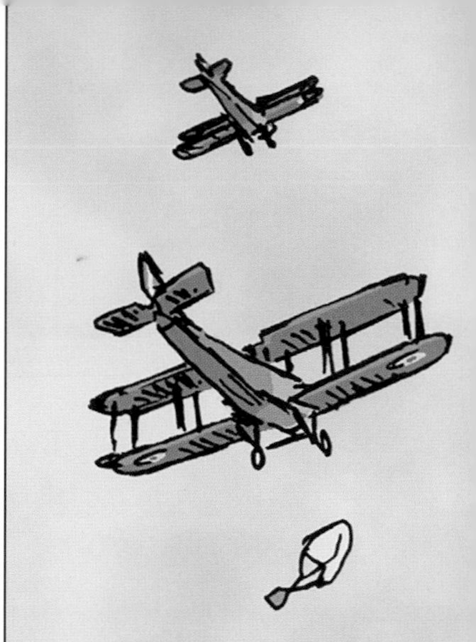

After the War

Because of his injuries, Cher Ami never flew again. He returned to the United States in April 1919. Reporters met him at the pier and spread his story of saving the Lost Battalion in newspapers and magazines.

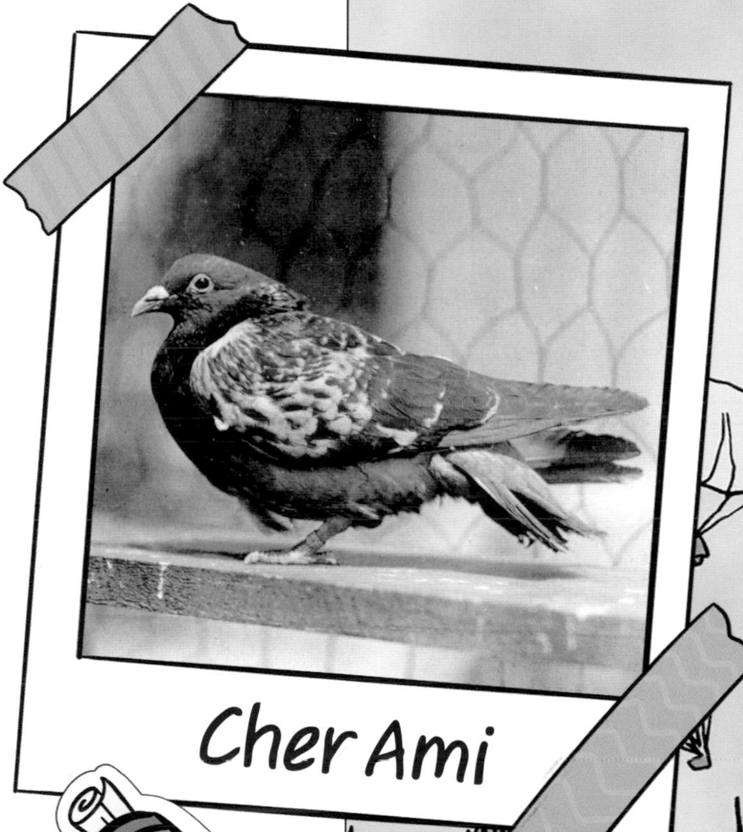
Cher Ami

However, the terrible wounds Cher Ami suffered on his historic flight took their toll. He died a few months after returning to America. His body was preserved and put on display at the Smithsonian Institute in June 1921. He became an instant hit with the public.

Cher Ami is currently on display at the new National Museum of History and Technology at the Smithsonian.

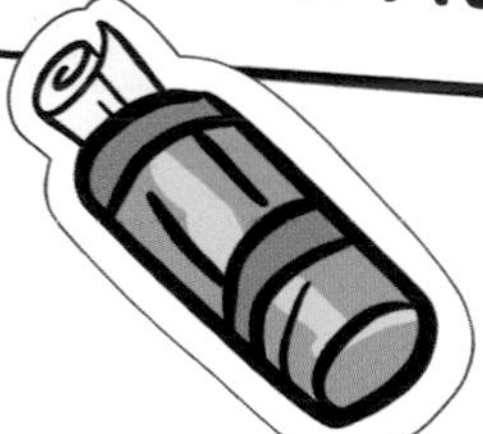

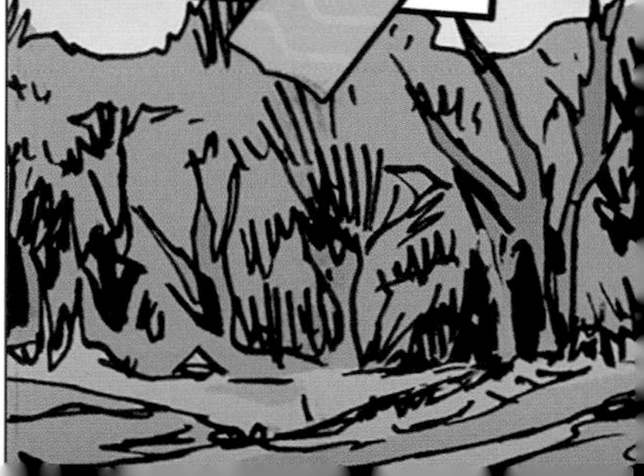

Glossary

alliance (uh-LY-uhnts)
an agreement between
two nations or groups of
people to work together

artillery (ar-TIL-ur-ee)
large, powerful guns that
are usually mounted
on wheels or another
supporting structure

assassinate
(uh-SASS-uh-nayt)
to murder a person who is
well-known or important

flank (FLANGK)
the far left or right side
of a group of soldiers

infantry (IN-fuhn-tree)
a group of soldiers trained
to fight and travel on foot

intercept (in-tur-SEPT)
to stop and capture
something that belongs to
an opponent

neutral (NOO-truhl)
not taking any side in
a war or disagreement

objective (uhb-JEK-tiv)
a goal or something you
are trying to achieve

rations (RASH-unz)
food supplied to armies
during a war

reinforcements
(ree-in-FORS-muhntz)
extra troops sent to
strengthen an army

summon (SUHM-uhn)
to request or command
someone to come to you

vulnerable
(VUHL-nur-uh-buhl)
in a weak position and
likely to be easily hurt
or attacked

Read More

Bausum, Ann. *Stubby the War Dog: The True Story of World War I's Bravest Dog.* Washington, D.C.: National Geographic, 2018.

Dickmann, Nancy. *The Horror of World War I.* North Mankato, MN: Capstone Press, 2018.

Henzel, Cynthia Kennedy. *Eyewitness to the Western Front.* Mankato, MN: Childs World, 2018.

Internet Sites

Britannica Kids: World War I
kids.britannica.com/kids/article/World-War-I/353933

DK Findout!: World War I
dkfindout.com/us/history/world-war-i/

Smithsonian: Cher Ami
si.edu/object/cher-ami%3Anmah_425415

National Museum U.S. Army: Cher Ami
thenmusa.org/biographies/cher-ami/

About the Author

Nel Yomtov is an award-winning author of children's nonfiction books and graphic novels. He specializes in writing about history, current events, biography, architecture, and military history. He has written numerous graphic novels for Capstone, including the recent *School Strike for Climate* and *Journeying to New Worlds: A Max Axiom Super Scientist Adventure*. In 2020 he self-published *Baseball 100*, an illustrated book featuring the 100 greatest players in baseball history. Nel lives in the New York City area.

About the Illustrator

Mark Simmons is a freelance illustrator and cartoonist based in San Francisco. His past work includes comics for publishers such as Capstone, Behrman House, and Rebellion, as well as animation and advertising storyboards, animated operas, and other strange things. He also teaches comic art, figure drawing, and wildlife illustration for local zoos, schools, and museums. He loves animals of all kinds, especially bugs! For more info, visit www.ultimatemark.com.